CREATING TECHNICAL MANUALS

CREATING TECHNICAL MANUALS
A Step-by-Step Approach to Writing User-Friendly Instructions

Donald H. Cunningham, Ph.D.
Professor of English &
Director of Technical and Professional Writing
Texas Tech University

Gerald Cohen

McGraw-Hill Book Company
New York St. Louis San Francisco Auckland
Bogotá Hamburg Johannesburg London Madrid
Mexico Montreal New Delhi Panama Paris
São Paulo Singapore Sydney Tokyo Toronto

Library of Congress Cataloging in Publication Data
Cunningham, Donald H.
    Creating technical manuals.

    Includes index.
    1. Technical writing.   2. Technical manuals.
I. Cohen, Gerald.   II. Title.
T11.C86 1984   808'.0666   83-25527
ISBN 0-07-011584-2

1234567890   DOC/DOC   8987654

ISBN 0-07-011584-2

The editors for this book were Patricia Allen-Browne and Nancy
Warren, the designer was Mark E. Safran, and the production
supervisor was Reiko F. Okamura. It was set in Sabon by Achorn
Graphics.

Printed and bound by R. R. Donnelley & Sons Company.

For my mother, Ethel McKee, with love—DHC
To my family, my inspiration: Geraldine, Claudette,
Theron, and Jeffrey—GIC

Contents

Preface

The purpose of this book is to help technical experts, writers, and editors create easy-to-follow instructions for specific readers to perform specific tasks. To simplify our presentation we use the term *manual* throughout this book to refer to any type of instructions—whether an instruction sheet on how to replace an automobile headlamp, a booklet on do-it-yourself plumbing, or a technical publication for a computerized accounting program.

The instructions may be for a particular commercial product (assembling, shipping, installing, operating, or repairing a Smash-O-Matic trash compactor, for example) or for performing a particular procedure regardless of the product (preparing a small animal for an electrocardiogram, how to get more money for a used car, or how to identify igneous rocks, for example). Thus a manual might explain how to repair Apex televisions or explain how to prepare and serve dinners to airline passengers.

If you are a writer with little or no technical background and little or no experience in writing manuals, you are our primary reader. This book will show you how to become a better creator of manuals than you ever imagined you could be, no matter how new you are to the field or how many times you have tried other approaches and failed.

Perhaps you have a technical background but little or no experience at writing manuals. You are also our reader. If you have to create a manual or work with a writer or editor to create a manual, this book will show you how to become a more knowledge-able collaborator with writers and editors by explaining how you can begin to think like they do. This should take the mystery out of how skilled manual writers create effective manuals.

If you are that rare exception—a writer who has good technical training and is an experienced creator of manuals—you are also our reader. This book will show you a rational, step-by-step approach that can help you become an even more efficient and happy writer. Even if you find only four or five ideas of practical value to you, this book will have served its purpose.

Why will the approach in this book succeed? Because it will help you overcome some of the biggest barriers that impede creating read-able and usable manuals: (1) the difficult and often confusing process of gathering, selecting, and presenting information when several per-sons are involved in the project; (2) the extraneous information and unclear lanaguage that finds its way into manuals, forcing the reader to direct enormous amounts of energy to finding needed information and to deciphering what statements mean; and (3) the "heavy" ap-pearance of text that obscures the nature of the instructions and makes it easy for the reader to lose track of the procedure.

This book explains a process that you can use when you create *any* manual—your next one, for instance. There are many ways to clas-sify manuals: according to the type of job—installation, mainte-nance, repair, overhaul, and so forth; according to the locations where they are used—in the office, in the field, in the repair depot, and in other places; according to whether the amount of informa-tion, the location of the work, or the number of procedures dictates a single- or a multivolume manual; according to their market—do-it-yourselfer or professional. While different types of information may be required at different user sites and different readers will need different information, all manuals have the same principal mission: to explain the proper way to work with new products or to perform procedures, usually for the first time. It is on this common goal of all manuals that we base our assumption that you can use our step-by-step approach for creating a manual regardless of its type.

Our fundamental assumption is that creating a manual is a pro-cess. To make that process rational and easy from beginning to end, we provide you with a series of plan sheets to help you do the right things in the right way. Of course, the plan sheets are not so important as the principles of effective communication behind them, but they help you keep those principles in mind *at all times*. The plan sheets also give you another advantage over more traditional ways of writing: you work with plan sheets, not blank pieces of paper or an empty video display screen.

The plan sheets help you create a manual from *scratch*. Everybody agrees that a manual must have clear, readable text and graphics; a table of contents, introduction, and index; and an attractive layout. But those are the results. How are they achieved? Most approaches separate the research from the writing stage and do not bridge the two very well. Woody Allen once said: "Getting from nothing to the first draft is the hardest part of writing." We agree. But we believe the plan sheets will help you through those difficult early stages—by showing you how to combine them in a way that lets you start creating from scratch. In effect, the plan sheets combine the research and writing into a single stage. By reading the introduction and Chapter 1, you will get a sense of how the process works. Chapters 2 to 4 explain how to use the plan sheets for gathering and presenting specific information.

In addition to explaining the process of creating manuals from scratch, this book focuses on those points of communication that make manuals more readable and usable. It deals with those questions that are uppermost in the reader's mind: What is the product or procedure? How does it work? How does it differ from other products or procedures? How do I use it? How do I get started? How do I fix it? A manual that answers these questions transforms an unqualified user into a competent operator. This book explains how to provide the information the reader needs to get the job done.

This book also shows you how to avoid the worst stylistic problem in manuals: jargon, which we call technical manual English, or TME. Readers of manuals often encounter a language the likes of which they have never read or heard—a strange language full of acronyms and buzzwords invented by persons insensitive to the idiom of our language. We believe that one language is suitable for all applications and all situations—plain English. No one has ever invented a better medium in our language for the communication of clear thought. We understand the necessity for legitimate technical terminology to make fine distinctions in highly technical or scientific treatises. But we believe that readers of manuals are distressed by unnecessarily abstract terms and phrases. Why write "Perform the X closure function" when "Close X" is just as good—even better? You will find in Chapters 2 to 6 our thoughts on how to use plain English in manuals.

Finally, in addition to describing a rational process for creating manuals and strategies for presenting relevant information in plain English, this book gives you some ideas about how to structure and package material graphically so the reader will be able to *see* how to do the job and will be able to follow complicated procedures without getting lost. In Chapters 3 to 5, you will find ways to help the reader thread his or her own way through troubleshooting procedures and other decision-making paths. In Chapter 6, you will find guidelines for applying these techniques to writing for the world of computers.

That is what this book is all about: showing you how to collect materials for creating manuals, how to write manuals in plain English, and how to structure and focus the presentation of complex material.

Gerald Cohen and Donald H. Cunningham

CREATING TECHNICAL MANUALS

Introduction

We are in the midst of what we regard as a crisis in manual writing. Earlier manuals (say, those published before 1970) were written to an audience which, for the most part, tolerated inferior writing as the norm. With current manuals, you are addressing an entirely new audience—a more sophisticated and liberated audience that will not tolerate a poorly conceived manual. In other words, what worked in the past will not work today. Why?

First, there is an increasing reluctance to read instructions, whether they are on a product, on its packaging, or in a manual. Why is that so? Is it human tendency? Is it the age of television we live in? Is it because the manuals of the past spawned a reputation for being written with little attempt to be clear or to be brief? Whatever the reason, you must face this reality and do something about it.

Second, people today are more discerning. They know that their inability to understand a manual is *not* a reflection on them but on those who created and published the manual.

Third, there is a need—as never before—to get the reader productive right away. The reader cannot, and will not, spare the time for a long period of learning for a product or procedure that is supposed to be simple and easy to use or do, maintain, or repair.

Anyone involved in technical operations and maintenance knows the most common defects of manuals that have led to this crisis. Too many manuals have the same unmistakable stamp, the

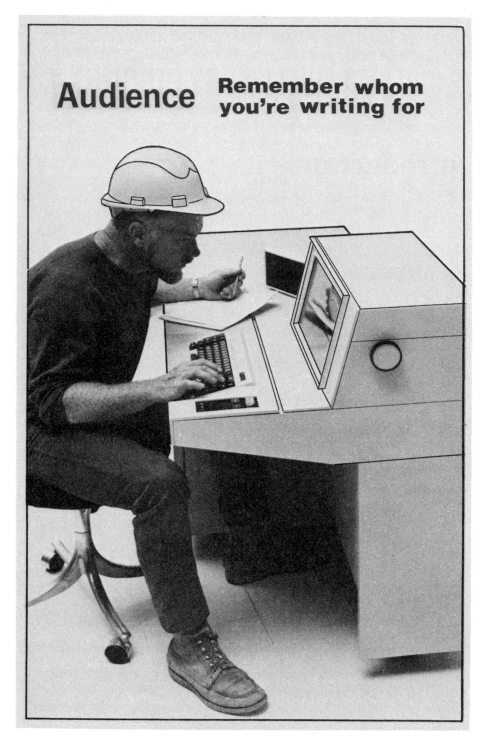

Fig. I-2 Get to the point. When you get into a cab, you want to be driven to your destination by the shortest, most direct route. When your readers open your manual, they want to get what they need in the fastest, most direct way.

same look: generally bad writing, information difficult to find, an absence of information where it should be, irrelevant information drowning relevant information, a lack of relevant information.

What is the solution? You should give as high a priority to improving the manuals as was given to improving the product or procedure itself. No document is likely to be more important to its reader. No document needs to be more clear-cut. It's like the solution to a math problem: it's either right or it's wrong. Half-right doesn't count. You can resolve to follow these eight general ground rules that will make manuals easier to read and understand. When you do, it will be a better day for you . . . and for your readers.

Fig. I-1 As you begin to design the manual, you need to know several things about its intended readers: How much do they already know about the procedure? How extensive a manual do they need? What level of language and what types of graphics are best for them? Do they have any aversions about performing certain procedures? Make sure that everything in the manual is tailored to the intended readers' needs. The more completely you can visualize readers using the manual, the better you can tailor the manual to them. (*Courtesy of International Business Machines Corporation*)

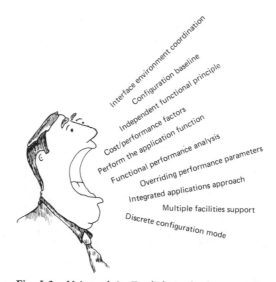

Fig. I-3 Using plain English is the best assurance that your manual will be understood by most readers. Plain English means writing "Calibrate X" rather than "Perform the calibrating function on X." The latter statement is an example of what we call technical manual English, the undesirably abstract expressions that have become one of the greatest impediments to readers' understanding manuals.

- Don't waste the beginning of the manual. Write it as though the reader will have only 20 minutes to give to the entire manual. This will ensure that the reader has a chance of reading the most important facts and ideas to be delivered.

- Write to get the reader productive as soon as possible. The reader can't spare the time for a long period of learning in today's world.

- Respect the reader's time. To ensure this, ask yourself these two questions:

  Is the reader likely to know this information? If the answer is yes, leave the information out.

  Does the reader really need to know this information to do the job? If the answer is yes, put the information in. If not, take it out.

  It's not hard to imagine what a strict application of these two tests would do to the bulk of many manuals. The manual must be

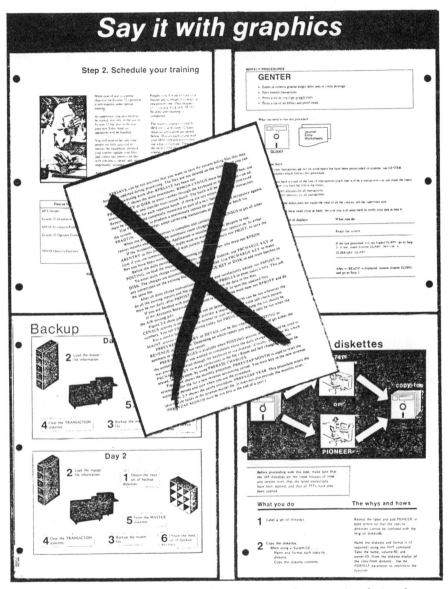

Fig. I-4 One of the most significant changes in manual preparation during the past 20 years is the increased use of graphics to show the reader how to do the job. Seeing is believing . . . and understanding. (*Reprinted by permission from International Business Machines Corporation*)

informative, but make the information earn its way into the manual.

- Remember that clear writing is simply good manners. Obscure writing is an intolerable discourtesy toward readers. Always make the manual as pleasant to read as possible. Reading a manual should not be like having root-canal work done.

- Don't merely *list* technical facts. They must be translated into ideas that are meaningful to the reader. Remember, nothing is self-explanatory. Never leave the reader stranded with a question like this in mind: "So the manual told me all about the Z file. Now what am I supposed to *do* about it?"

- Bridge from the old to the new, from the known to the unknown. Don't drop the reader into the middle of something new without explaining how it relates to what she or he already knows.

- In its organization, its presentation, and its language, make the manual *instructional*. State specific instructions in command language, in the imperative mood. But remember not to confuse the language of discussion and description with the language of instruction.

- *Show* rather than tell the reader *how* to do it. Make graphics equal partners with text. Curtailing either usually impedes communication.

If we were to reduce these ground rules to a bare-bones minimum, these four points (as illustrated in Figures I-1 to I-4) would remain:

Remember your reader
Get to the point
Stick to plain English
Say it with graphics

Once you begin applying these ideas, you will start producing dividends: the beginning of the manual will be meaningful, useful, and pleasant to read; the bulk of the manual will be cut, because the only information in it helps the reader to *do* something; the reading will be easy because the instructions are clear; the format of the manual will be a map. Everybody's job will be easier, especially the reader's.

Developing a Procedure That Works

In every manual writing project in which you are likely to be involved, there are three personalities. The following vignette and Figure 1-1 depict their plight.

They didn't say in the books that it would be like this, the writer thought, sitting at a desk which was covered with stacks of handwritten notes, typed engineering reports, schematic drawings, and computer printouts. These books had said to collect and study available information, confer with the technical staff, make a preliminary outline, write and revise, and proofread. No, there wasn't anything in the books about having to work through all this material that nobody but an expert could understand.

Before working much longer, the writer—wadding another sheet of paper—looks up and says,

"I need help."

An engineer-designer, pointing to the stack of material on the writer's desk, replies,

"I've given you everything you need right there."

Looking up from a manual toward the writer, a reader says,

"You think you need help!"

The publication dilemma

"I gave you all the info you need—tons of it. It's right there on your desk: my logs, the printouts, the specs, the lab reports, the drawings . . ."

The engineer

"I can't make heads or tails out of it . . ."

"I don't know what *you* need . . ."

"I need help!"

The writer

"You think *you* need help!"

"I don't know. Period!"

The reader

Fig. 1-1 Your most important *writing* job is to translate the material you receive into information that is meaningful to your readers.

Each personality has its problem.

The writer, who must gather the information, choose the appropriate format, and translate the information into the reader's language—whatever that might be—is likely to be relatively unfamiliar with the subject matter and unable to devote the time it would take to become a subject-matter expert. She or he usually has no set procedure for gathering the information or making the many decisions about content, organization, format, and style required for the manual. There may be no reliable or valid way of assessing how effectively the finished manual communicates with its intended reader.

The subject-matter experts—the project engineers and technicians who are the primary source of technical information for the manual—may have few writing skills and little literary ambition, and may not really know what the writer needs in the first place. Familiar with the complexities of the technology, they lose sight of the reader and assume that everyone automatically understands the special terms of their field. Also, they find writing painful. Often pushed reluctantly into providing text for the manual, their solution is to write as little as possible and get it over with quickly, supplying perhaps only the product specifications and schematic and assembly diagrams—information written earlier for other purposes and readers other than those who will actually use the manual.

The reader, who turns to the manual expecting help on how to do the job, and who may be confronted by several dozen—or several hundred—pages of boring, irrelevant, and confusing material, is, of course, not even present during the preparation and production of the manual. Out of sight, out of mind.

So the trouble starts right at the beginning. It is like this in nearly every manual writing project in which you may be involved.

Once you are assigned the task, you must find some course of action that will enable you to create the manual. How do you get the information? How do you translate the information so that the reader gets what is wanted or needed? How do you assess the effectiveness of the manual?

To overcome these obstacles and solve these problems, you must work closely with the subject-matter experts and represent the reader. But you must also *control* the situation. You must remain in your sphere of expertise, for no one will be able to communicate as well as you can. Likewise, the subject-matter experts must remain in their spheres of expertise, for no one will ever know the subject matter as well as the experts know it. But you are the one who must lead the collaboration. If you fail, the manual will be a failure. Just as the product engineer is responsible for the quality of the product, you are responsible for the quality of the contents, format, and style of the manual that supports the product.

So, like it or not, you are responsible. In creating a manual, you undertake a large and diverse set of tasks. Your ability to exercise control (in a collaborative manner, of course) over these tasks spells the difference between success and failure. Your success depends upon your developing a procedure that involves four interrelated activities:

1. Developing documentation priorities that ensure that your efforts produce a readable and usable manual.
2. Using plan sheets to gather the information you need to write the first draft of the manual.
3. Setting performance objectives to clarify the purpose of the manual and each part of the manual.
4. Collaborating with subject-matter experts in a way that is comfortable for them and for you.

DEVELOPING DOCUMENTATION PRIORITIES

Your first step in developing a sound approach to creating a manual is to arrange your documentation priorities, ordering them according to the needs of your readers. This leads to criteria that will give the highest priority to the features of communication that most help the reader.

The criteria should be concerned with such questions as:

- Is this passage relevant? (Would its removal be detrimental to the purpose of the manual?)
- Is it economical of the reader's time? (Does it take a long time to express a very simple thought?)

Priority level	Feature of quality of the manual	Skill and intellectual effort required of publications people
Highest	Understandable (does it communicate?)	Highest
	Usable (does it work?)	
	Filled with specific examples	
	Readable (not painful)	
	Specific and to the point (not overly general)	
	Logically organized	
	Well-paced, not dense	
	Visually pleasant	
	Uncomplicated (in writing and appearance)	
	Varied in sentence structure and length	
	Correct grammar	
	Correct punctuation	
	Correct spelling	
Lowest	Conforms to publication specifications	Lowest

Fig. 1-2 You need to establish documentation priorities that will produce the best possible manual for your readers. Everything, including such mechanical matters as spelling and capitalization, is important in the final version of the manual. But certain features, such as comprehensibility, are far more important in determining the usefulness of the manual. Give the highest priority to them.

- Is it written well? (Or is it boring, pretentious, and stereotypical?)
- Does it work? (By following the instructions in the manual, can the reader do the job?)

As you can see in Figure 1-2, working with these criteria will encourage you to apply your intellectual and creative skills where they are most needed. The first ten features are the most important, and certainly spelling, punctuation, and grammar should conform to good usage. Putting publication specifications at the bottom of the list may seem unnatural to you, and so let's make a few observations about the nature of publication specifications.

As a writer, you have a source that you often turn to—in fact, feel compelled to respond to—the publication specifications for a certain kind of manual. Specifications, of course, can be helpful, especially if they are clear and complete (without being overspecified) and if they are designed for exactly the kind of manual you have to create. But specifications don't always help, because while they identify what information to include, they do not show how to include it or how to relate it to the reader's needs. Specifications identify the contents of the finished manual, but they don't really help you create the manual from scratch. They are concerned with writing as a product, not with writing as a process. Equally troublesome, specifications are usually oriented to the company and its products, not to the job or the reader. So slavishly adhering to publication specifications won't guarantee a good manual.

Don't forget that publication specifications probably were originally written several years (if not decades) ago by people like yourself. Therefore, you should not regard them as sacred and unchangeable. All too often, once specifications are written and printed, they take on an immortality of some kind. Just remember that they, like anything else, may not be completely appropriate for the task at hand; they may be outmoded and need revising. If this is the case, bring the problem to the attention of those who have the authority to change the specifications. If your case is strong, the chances are good that you can get the specifications modified. Always read the specifications carefully and determine whether you need to negotiate with your customer to modify them in order to give the customer a usable manual.

USING PLAN SHEETS

A house can be built without a set of blueprints, but if it is, nobody will be sure until after it's built that the bathroom wasn't put on the wrong side of the house, or that there wasn't some other goof, such as having two doors banging against each other or a refrigerator door opening into the path of traffic into the kitchen.

Just as a house should not be built without a blueprint, a manual should not be created without a blueprint—not just an outline, but a blueprint. A set of blueprints for a house specifies objectives from the potential homeowner's point of view. For a manual, the blueprint reflects the potential reader's point of view, closely matching what the reader needs.

When a manual is being created, the ultimate reader is not even in the picture. You, of course, are supposed to keep the reader in mind, but in effect the reader is missing. So you must *assert* the reader's presence. In short, you serve as an agent representing the reader. One of the great failures of manual writing is the lack of representation of the reader's needs.

You will find it helpful to use the plan sheets presented in this book to record certain information for the manual—information that the reader needs.

- *Plan Sheet A:* Naming the Product or Procedure
- *Plan Sheet B:* What the Product or Procedure Does
- *Plan Sheet C:* Translating Technical Facts
- *Plan Sheet D:* The Distinguishing Characteristics of the Product or Procedure
- *Plan Sheet E:* The Old Product or Procedure
- *Plan Sheet F:* The New Product or Procedure
- *Plan Sheet G:* The Task Outline Sheet
- *Plan Sheet H:* The Task Detail Sheet
- *Plan Sheet I:* The Alternatives Sheet
- *Plan Sheet J:* The Troubleshooting Table

Throughout this book, there are blank plan sheets which you are encouraged to reproduce or redesign for your specific purposes. These forms are intended to guide you in following the procedures and techniques explained here for creating a technical manual. These plan sheets may seem like odd devices to you, but they should help you overcome many of the obstacles encountered in getting the information you need from the subject-matter experts. They are labor-saving devices for you. The plan sheets, which are filled out in collaboration with or by the subject-matter experts, serve as blueprints for different parts of the manual.

The advantages of the plan sheets will become obvious when you start using them. The subject-matter experts fill them out instead of writing a conventional manuscript. The plan sheets indicate what information you need and encourage the subject-matter experts to provide it in a form that is close to the coherent pattern you will use in writing the manual. With the completed plan sheets, you will be able to determine systematically and with reasonable completeness the information you need to write the parts of the manual.

SETTING PERFORMANCE OBJECTIVES

Each Plan Sheet H: The Task Detail Sheet will be designed around a performance objective. Establishing clear performance objectives—stating what the reader will be able to do—should be one of your earliest and highest priorities. It is important that the objectives be measurable so that you can observe whether the reader achieves the objectives, that is, whether he or she can do the job. An objective such as "the reader will understand how to install an air eliminator tank on the bulk plant meter line" cannot be measured readily. How would you measure *understanding*? The objective "the reader will be able to install an air eliminator tank on a bulk plant meter line in 2 hours" can be measured, because you can observe the reader and tell whether he or she can perform the task within the specified time.

Among others, one source for the idea of performance objectives is the work of Robert F. Mager, who emphasized the importance of preparing instructional objectives in teaching. As you continue to read this book, you may also want to read Mager's *Preparing Instructional Objectives* (Fearon Press, Belmont, California, 1962). Although it is not mandatory that you read Mager's book, we believe you will benefit from it, and you might see other implications for your writing. Mager's approach to defining educational objectives has direct implications for writing manuals. If we substitute the words *writer, reader,* and *manual* for Mager's *instructor, student,* and *educational unit,* the parallel is seen easily. Part of our approach to writing step-by-step instructions in Chapter 3 is derived from the work of Mager and Kenneth M. Beach, Jr., in their *Developing Vocational Instruction* (Fearon Press, Belmont, California, 1967).

USING SUBJECT-MATTER EXPERTS

You cannot dispense with subject-matter experts, usually designers, engineers, or technicians, as your primary sources of information. What you can do is make it easier for them to give you the information you need to write the manual. You cannot expect the subject-matter experts to write the manual. That's *your* job.

Remember these three things about subject-matter experts:

1. Most will not have time to provide data in reasonably well written form.
2. Some even resent the time-consuming discussions often necessary to give you what you need to know about the subject.
3. If they provide information in traditional manuscript form, you usually have to rework it extensively.

As a result, use the plan sheets (the blueprints) to help you get the information you need. It is important, though, to remember that you may sometimes have to persist in getting the subject-matter experts to give you the information. They are busy people.

The plan sheets will help get the manual launched by enabling the subject-matter experts to supply information that is relevant, graphic, and usable in a form that is comfortable for them. They will soon realize that filling out the plan sheets is easier than writing conventional manuscripts, with all the work entailed and frustration inherent in that process.

Once the plan sheets are properly and completely filled out, you have more than half the job done—maybe 60 to 70 percent. You have source material that is more useful and informative than anything you have ever worked with before. You are now free to apply the inventiveness, the imagination, and the creativity so lacking in conventional manuscripts. The actual task of writing should go quickly and routinely. You now have a good chance to create a manual that is superior in many respects to the manuals of the past.

TWO

Explaining What the Product or Procedure Is

Pick up any manual and read its beginning. Most likely it has the same stamp and look as its predecessors: it introduces the subject by a string of stereotyped sentences written in such abstract and general language that you can't tell one product or procedure from another.

Does the manual's introduction clearly state what the product or procedure does? Its purpose? Its distinguishing characteristics? Does it tell how the new product or procedure relates to the old or familiar? If it doesn't, how then are readers supposed to "get a handle" on what the new product or procedure is?

Readers can understand new data or new ideas only when they can relate them to what they already know or have experience with. Not having a bridge to cross from the old to the new handicaps readers who are trying to understand the unfamiliar. If you don't begin by writing to their needs and level of understanding, how can you ask them to read your manuals?

What can you do to construct a good introduction? You can give readers a basic understanding of the product or procedure by describing its function and distinguishing characteristics in clear, concise language that relates *to the readers for whom the manual is designed*. And you should convey that understanding quickly. First impressions are usually lasting, and generally you'll be given only two or three pages to prove that your manual is worth reading.

The aspects of the product or procedure that readers most likely need to understand fall into three categories. Here's a brief introduction to them; the rest of the chapter discusses each in greater detail.

1.   *What the product or procedure is called.* It is obvious to even the most casual reader that products and procedures have curious names (e.g., MLT 639A—as if we spoke only in letters and numbers—or Integrated Communication System Facility—as if we used only words that were pulled down from some ethereal realm). Even if you have little opportunity to help name the product or procedure, you can play an important role in establishing effective nomenclature that will make the manual more meaningful to its users.

2.   *What the product or procedure does.* There seems to be a reluctance to say what a product or procedure does, for we have observed a writing habit that may be called "detouring." It is the habit of constantly emphasizing the *potential* for a thing or action rather than saying straight out that the product or procedure *does* it (as Figure 2-1 illustrates). Detouring results in an unnatural, stilted prose where the only verbs are *provides, performs,* or three or four other equally abstract verbs. This is poor use of a language that derives its power and effectiveness from its vast inventory of verbs.

We've never been able to understand fully this placing such emphasis on potential or capability. It is caused partly by the designer's or inventor's tendency to think abstractly of the potential of a product or procedure while it is still in the embryonic "thought" stage. It is also caused partly by persons who tend to think primarily of the "capability" of the product or procedure. One of them explained it this way: "You can't say 'It detects amplified noise impulses,' because there may be times when it doesn't." That's what we call Fort Worth reasoning, named for a Fort Worth customer who left this note for the paper carrier: "Don't leave a paper today. Of course, when I say today I mean tomorrow, because I am writing this yesterday."

You can help readers immensely by making them aware of exactly what the product or procedure does, rather than by discussing abstractly or theoretically its potential or capability.

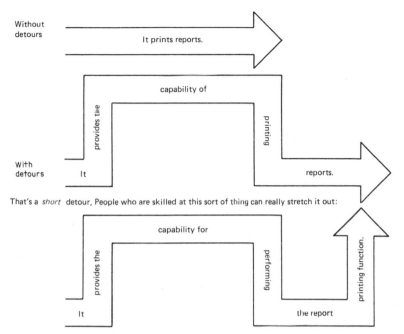

Fig. 2-1 Verbal detours, such as unnecessarily abstract verbs and nouns, create tortuously long sentences. Get to the point with concrete, specific words that create mental images in the minds of your readers.

3. *How the product or procedure differs from other products or procedures.* It helps your readers understand when you relate the new to the old, when you bridge from the known to the unknown. That's basically how we learn new things. Otherwise, your readers have no way of associating the new product or procedure with something they are already familiar with. Here are some fragments that will help you phrase your own bridging statements.

> Machine X is versatile. It not only reads optical characters (like machine Y), but it also reads fingerprints (unlike machine Y).
>
> Like machine X, machine Y converts. . . . Like machine X, it runs. . . . Unlike machine X, however, machine Y cannot. . . .
>
> As an instrument for recording blood pressure, the X product offers several advantages over Y machines:
> • It saves time by. . . .
> • It saves effort by. . . .

- It is more accurate because. . . .
- It is easier to use because. . . .

In other words, you must answer such questions as: Why is it better? How does it differ from older equipment, methods, procedures, products? What is it like? What is it unlike? What does it look like? How does it work?

NAMING THE PRODUCT OR PROCEDURE

You can make a useful contribution as early as when decisions are being made about nomenclature, for the meaninglessness that accompanies much documentation begins as early as the stage of naming the product and its parts or the procedure and its steps.

Technical manual English (TME) is a language found only in written form and only in technical or instructional literature. It usually can be heard only when it is being read aloud from a manual. It is the opposite of plain English. Consider, for example, a name such as "Functional Interactive Dynamic Interface." Can you guess what it is from its name? Can you imagine reading the name several times? Even if shortened to the acronym FIDI, the name becomes just another ugly acronym in a literature already overflowing with ugly acronyms.

Ponderous names are only one example of TME. Verbs, usually passive, also play a part. Let's see how TME compares with plain English:

TME	PLAIN ENGLISH
Frequency channel selecting device.	Frequency selector.
Nonstructural mitigating alternatives to flood control.	Relocating some buildings out of the flood zone and elevating other buildings so water cannot reach the main floor.
The RF signal amplification function is performed by the FET-1 and its associated circuitry.	FET-1 and its associated circuitry amplify the RF signal.
The operator must perform a manual answer.	Answer the telephone.

The meaningless phrases that make up TME are created by the *overuse* of abstract words and of passive voice constructions. This is not to say that abstract words and the passive voice should be outlawed from our language. We often find ourselves using both, for good reasons. The point is, we should avoid using them *unnecessarily*.

On the subject of abstract words, H. W. Fowler wrote:

> Turgid, flabby English is full of abstract nouns; the commonest ending of abstract nouns is *-tion,* and to count the *-tion* words in what one has written, or, better, to cultivate an ear that without special orders challenges them as they come, is one of the simplest and most effective means of making oneself less unreadable.[1]

The technological revolution of the last 100 years has brought with it a host of new abstract terms. Unfortunately, many such names were introduced by persons who didn't know the rules for creating new words out of an already existing vocabulary. The consequences of overusing abstract words are clearly described by Bergen and Cornelia Evans:

> The more abstract a word is, the more objects it refers to and the less it tells us about them. The more specific a word is, the more information it conveys. It is very easy to use words that are too general. In fact, this is the most obvious characteristic of ineffective writing. A good writer fits his words as closely as possible to his meaning. He will use *container* only if he is talking about several containers. If he is talking about a barrel, he will call it a barrel.[2]

When subject-matter experts and writers are afflicted by TME, they tend not only to call a barrel a *container,* but go beyond that and call it a *functional transportation module* (FTM, of course).

Special care must be taken when you name products and procedures or you will be writing in TME. By learning how things have been named traditionally, you can avoid the pitfalls of TME. It is difficult to write about products and procedures that have been labeled with TME names. (Can you imagine having to refer to "Functional Interactive Dynamic Interface" or "Functional Interac-

---

[1] *A Dictionary of Modern English Usage,* 2d ed., Oxford University Press, London, 1965, p. 640.

[2] *A Dictionary of Contemporary American Usage,* Random House, Inc., New York, 1957, p. 6.

tive Dynamic Interface Facility" dozens of times?) It's even worse to read about them.

Let's consider just three of the traditional methods of creating new names.

First, especially in the sciences, a thing might be named for its inventor or discoverer. Examples: *ohm* for Georg Ohm; *ampere* for André-Marie Ampère; *Wangensteen suction* for Owen H. Wangensteen, an American surgeon who invented a suction machine to use in the treatment of gastric and intestinal disorders. The Fahrenheit, Kelvin, and Celsius scales are named after the scientists who invented them.

Second, usually by adding an agent suffix (*-er, -or*), a thing might be named by telling what it does. Thus, a machine that typewrites is called a *typewriter;* a machine that processes words is called a word *processor;* a machine that refrigerates, a *refrigerator;* a machine that computes, a *computer.* A *percolator* is a specific kind of coffeemaker.

Third, a thing might be named for what it looks like. If it looks like a box, it is called a _____ box. Examples: *cash box* (note how concrete the name is; from it we know not only its shape, but its function); *icebox* (again shape and function); *cardboard box* (we see its shape and what it is made of). Can you visualize the appearance of a programming comb or a mushroom anchor or the appearance and operation of a caterpillar gate?

Note the concreteness of the second and third methods of naming.

Now let's consider the way things often seem to be named today. The names of many familiar objects and procedures incorporate buzzwords such as *system* and *facility* to make them sound more important. Thus, a printer or a refrigerator is now a *printing system* or *refrigerator system.* A building is now a *capital facility.* Laboratories have been replaced by *laboratory facilities* (maybe even *laboratory systems facilities*); libraries by *learning resource centers* or *library facilities* or *library facility complexes.* An announcement on a college bulletin board was recently changed from "Economics Tutoring" to "Economics Tutoring Laboratory." It won't be long, we surmise, until it reads "Economics Tutoring Laboratory System," then "Economics Tutoring Laboratory Systems Facility." A series of activities that once passed as *budgeting, budget planning,* or *financial planning* now are cloaked in the white tie and tails of *financial plan-*

ning function, financial planning operations, financial planning process, financial planning function process, or the inevitable *financial planning function process system.* This is how TME progresses.

There's nothing wrong with the word *system* or *facility* (or any other abstract word), but all too often such perfectly good words are rendered useless by misapplication in TME. They become abstract appendages giving weight to words that do not need it. Such words blur sharp distinctions and become what Ernest Gowers calls "shapeless bundles of uncertain content." Eventually, they come to mean nothing at all—a situation described in this statement by George Willis many years ago:

> It is true that one name can serve for many things, yet there is a limit to the principle of flexibility in nomenclature; words are surprisingly elastic, yet they have a breaking-point. If a name is required to mean too much, it will end by meaning nothing.[3]

This threat of extinction is especially true of abstract words, for, as Willis states, "every name must convey some definite, sensible image, or else it conveys nothing, and no person knows the meaning of any word unless he knows what sensible image it conveys or once conveyed."[4] What happens, for instance, to our understanding of *typewriter* if the name is changed to *type facilitator* or *type facilitating device* or *type systematizer*? Can we be sure we know what is meant by *typing facilities*? Are they the typewriters themselves? The typists? The rooms for the typewriters? The supplies for the typewriters and typists? All of the above? In Willis's words, it is difficult

> to apprehend the ideas which these [abstract] words convey without the mediation of some sensible image; once a word becomes disconnected with the sensible image with which it was formerly connected it becomes useless, a mere encumbrance to the language, a piece of dropsical verbiage, a pitfall to the careful thinker, a cloak of sham learning, pseudo-science and all manner of imposture.[5]

[3]*The Philosophy of Speech,* George Allen & Unwin, Ltd., London, 1919, p. 31.
[4]Ibid., p. 68.
[5]Ibid., p. 69.

Again, the word *system* can illustrate the trouble of using such words to name things. Thanks to our unending abuse of this innocent word, we have such TME absurdities as these titles of manuals:

| Systems Approach to Management Systems, Systems Generation

or

| *Systems Operating System: Systems Analyst Guide*

That's what we get when we name everything _____ *systems* or *systems* _____. We wind up writing prose that sounds like double-talk:

> These systems, in conjunction with the business planning system, provide an upward compatible family of transfer communications systems, providing a common applications program system. They facilitate the implementation of operations-oriented applications systems and provide an upward information system to the systems management system.

Imagine the problem your readers will have reading passages like that.

How did we reach this point where we are all splashing around in a swamp of rotten verbiage? Part of the problem is that we are locked into it; given the proliferation of "systems" and "facilities" in engineering and management—and the general infatuation with general systems theory—we can hardly avoid TME. After all, when everything you're writing about bears an abstract name, how can you find your way back to earth? How can you write readable prose intended for human beings if the things you must discuss bear unnecessarily abstract names?

But here is the real danger: we are becoming so anesthetized by this kind of linguacide that we don't even realize the damage we are doing to ourselves. A story that Al Kelly, the late grand comedian of double-talk, used to tell is revealing. Kelly, so the story goes, once posed as a physician at a medical meeting and reported to a group of doctors that he had been able to "rehabilitate patients by daily injections of triprobe into the right differnarium which translucentizes the stoline producing a black greel which enables you to stame the klob." Kelly said that there was "one thing disturbing me when I said that—some of the doctors were agreeing with me!"

We believe the same kind of thing is happening in manual writing. To verify our suspicions, we've conducted various experiments. In one, we took a passage, blanked out the name of the product it was talking about, brought it back to the group that distributed it, and asked them what it was that was being defined. Here it is, your typical TME passage:

> _____ is a highly responsive transaction-oriented data base—data communications interface between PBGK-4400 and user-written application programs. It is designed primarily for inquiry and transaction processing applications, but provides many of the facilities necessary to implement other terminal applications such as message switching and administrative handling.

Can you fill in the blank? Neither could anyone in the group, including the original writer.

What does all this mean? It means that continued reliance on abstract words not only lets a person write TME that baffles readers, but it may even let that same person write without knowing what is being said. This is the main indictment against TME.

Let's have a last word about the word _system_. It seems harmless enough, but through our infatuation with it in TME, we've turned it into a dead string of six letters. By contrast, if we said the word _paragraph_ to you, you would have at least some idea of what it means and how it relates to other things; that is, you would know that a paragraph is generally bigger than an alphabetical letter, a word, or a sentence, but usually smaller than a page, a chapter, or a book. You would know right away how it fits into the scheme of things.

Now suppose we say to you _multifunctional interactive communication system_. Do you have any sensible image of what it is? Is it a printed circuit you can hold in your hand? Is it an array of huge machines occupying three floors of a building? Or is it a vast network stretching across the United States? You simply have no idea, because the name itself is a string of abstract words joined together in prefabricated pomposity. Actually, it could be a TME term for *writing*.

Figures 2-2 and 2-3 make clear the necessity for keeping relationships well defined and easily separable. Note that in TME, where everything tends to be called _____ *system,* we don't have the hierarchy of meaning that enables us to grasp how things relate.

You should start early in encouraging the subject-matter experts to use familiar, concrete language that appeals directly to our stock of sensory impressions, and that recalls vividly to mind things we have seen, heard, tasted, touched, smelled; language which is close, in other words, to experience itself. Helping the subject-matter experts name the product or procedure sensibly is a good way to start documentation.

Use Plan Sheet A: Naming the Product or Procedure (Figure 2-4) to help you and the subject-matter experts name the product or procedure. This plan sheet is useful and easy to use. It helps you choose between several traditional ways of naming things: by what the thing does, by what it looks like, by blending words, by easily pronounced acronyms, and by favorably connotative words. While we do not wish to encourage the unnecessary creation of new acronyms, we recognize it as a valid form of naming. The filled-out sample Plan Sheet A (Figure 2-5) gives examples of effective naming.

EXPLAINING WHAT THE PRODUCT OR PROCEDURE DOES

Plan Sheet B: What the Product or Procedure Does (see Figure 2-8) is the simplest of all the plan sheets to fill out, for it contains only a brief explanation (usually a sentence will do) of what the product or procedure does. Before actually filling out Plan Sheet B, however, consider the language you will use in your explanation. It should contain no TME language detours. State clearly and concisely what the product or procedure does, avoid these detours by using concrete language, and write in the active voice as much as possible.

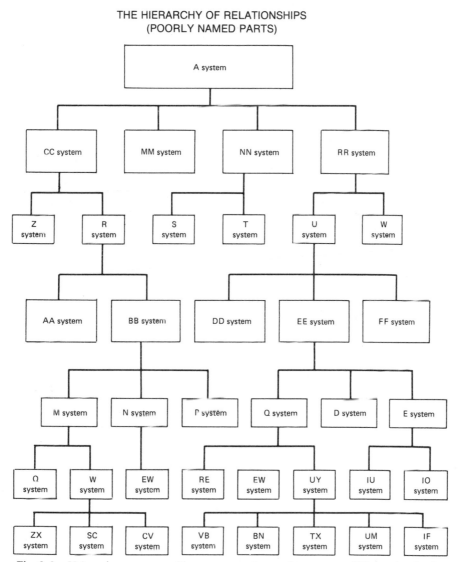

Fig. 2-2 Using abstract terms like *system, unit, routine* to name different levels of a procedure or process makes it difficult for readers to distinguish between those different levels.

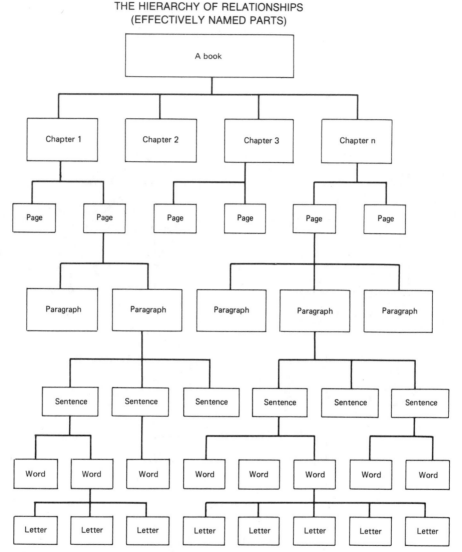

THE HIERARCHY OF RELATIONSHIPS
(EFFECTIVELY NAMED PARTS)

Fig. 2-3 In naming steps and substeps or parts and subparts, use words that help readers see the hierarchy of relationships.

PLAN SHEET A:
NAMING THE PRODUCT OR PROCEDURE

- By what it does

It	1: Action word	2: Object of action	=	2	1
			=		
			=		

- By what it looks like

Modifier	Noun	=	Name
		=	
		=	

- By blending words

First element	Second element	=	Name

- By easily pronounced acronyms

	=	

- By popular names having the psychological effect of favorable connotation

Fig. 2-4 Plan Sheet A: Naming the Product or Procedure.

PLAN SHEET A:
NAMING THE PRODUCT OR PROCEDURE

- By what it does

It	1: Action word	2: Object of action	=	2	1
It	prints	reports	=	report	printer
It	aligns	channels	=	channel	aligner

- By what it looks like

Modifier	Noun	=	Name
flat	car	=	flatcar
hair	spring	=	hairspring

- By blending words

First element Second element	=	Name
transfer resistor trans- + -istor	=	transistor
(Gr.) *tele* + (Gr.) *skopein* (distance) (to watch) "to watch the distance"	=	telescope
(Gr.) *xeros* + (Gr.) *graphikos* (dry) (drawing) "dry drawing"	=	xerography

- By easily pronounced acronyms

*s*elf-contained *u*nderwater *b*reathing *a*pparatus	=	scuba
*ra*dio *d*etecting *a*nd *r*anging	=	radar

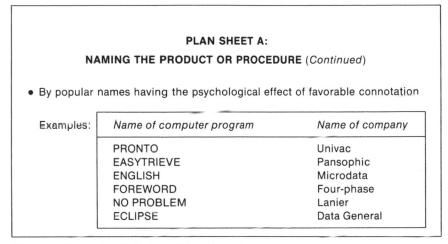

PLAN SHEET A:

NAMING THE PRODUCT OR PROCEDURE (Continued)

- By popular names having the psychological effect of favorable connotation

Examples:

Name of computer program	Name of company
PRONTO	Univac
EASYTRIEVE	Pansophic
ENGLISH	Microdata
FOREWORD	Four-phase
NO PROBLEM	Lanier
ECLIPSE	Data General

Fig. 2-5   Example of filled-out Plan Sheet A.

The Language Detours of TME

Since every product or procedure works in a predictable manner, it seems natural that we could state simply and clearly what it *does*. But abstract TME language—that pernicious infestation that plagues the terminology of manuals—can stretch a simple four-word statement of the product's function into fifteen words, with no increase in meaning, as shown in Figure 2-6.

Anyone who does much reading of manuals is struck by a startling realization: none of the products work! They merely *provide the capability* for doing the work. What actually does the work is never disclosed. If you apply the phrase *provides the capability* (it's almost always some form of the verb *provide*), you begin to see how odd this situation is. Allow us to exaggerate slightly to elaborate upon this point.

Does a bulb light?	No. It merely *provides the capability* of lighting.
Does a car run?	Seldom. It just *provides the capabilities* of running.
Does a vending machine dispense drinks?	No. It *provides the capability* of dispensing drinks. Or it *provides the capability of providing* drinks.

| The 3211 prints reports. | The 3211 can print reports. | The 3211 is capable of printing reports. | The 3211 provides the capability of printing reports. | The 3211 provides the capability of performing report printing. | The 3211 provides the capability of performing the report printing function. | The 3211 is a device which provides the capability of performing the report printing function. |

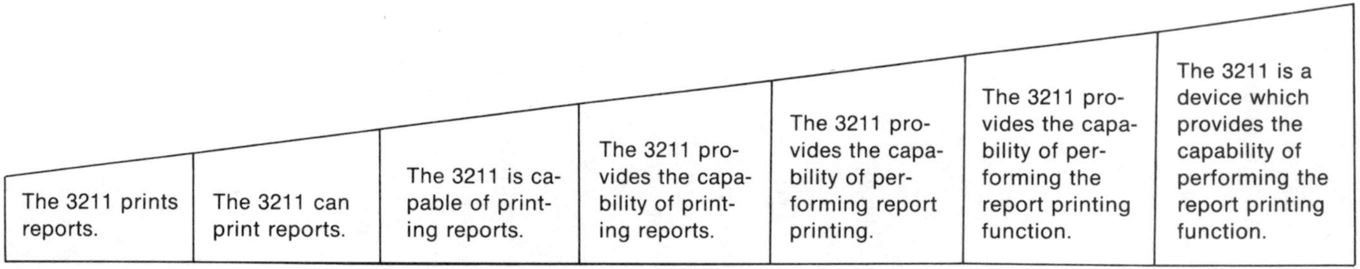

Fig. 2-6 How four words grow to fifteen, with no increase in meaning.

| Does System X monitor data from sensors? | Almost never. System X *provides the capability* of monitoring data. Or—even more noncommital—System X is *designed to provide* the capability of monitoring data (which suggests that sometimes we fall short of even *providing the you-know-what*). |

In this unreal literature of *provided capabilities,* nothing ever works, nothing ever moves, nothing ever does anything. And yet, standing in a machine shop, you could swear you see spindles turning, lathes cutting, material moving, products being shaped.

You wonder.

Although we gave those examples tongue-in-cheek, the problem is serious. Figure 2-7 shows just a few variations of TME language detours that exist in manuals we have studied. Except for four of them, these examples are written in the active voice. The writer can introduce another turn in the detour by unnecessarily using the passive voice.

Unfortunately, you are already stuck with dozens of abstract words because they were used to name the things and activities you must write about. So try to avoid thoughtlessly introducing even more abstractions.

Removing the TME Language Detours

Take a typical page of your own writing or that of the subject-matter experts you're working with and survey it to gauge its level of abstraction.

Here's how.

1. Circle all abstract nouns. Recognizing such words is not always easy. So, to simplify matters, here is a guideline that should be valid far more often than not: count all words ending in *-ance, -ence, -ity, -ment, -tion, -ure,* including their plurals. Also circle such abstract words as *area, aspect, basis, concept, factor, support, system, unit,* including their plurals. There may be other words that you want to include from your own experience. For

Without detours	Typical detours
The program converts files into datasets.	The program (allows, permits, enables, supports, performs) the file-dataset conversion function.
	The program (is used for, is designed for, is utilized for, is provided for, may be used for, provides the means for) file-dataset conversion.
	The program provides the capability of performing the file-dataset conversion function.
	The program provides the user with the capability of performing the file-dataset conversion function.
	File/dataset conversion capability is supported.
	The program supports file/dataset conversion.
	The program provides the capability for implementing the file-dataset conversion function.
	The program includes the functional capability of file-dataset conversion.
	Provision for file-dataset conversion is included.
	Program support for file-dataset conversion is provided.
	File-dataset conversion requirements are performed by the program.
	and so on.

Fig. 2-7 The language detours of technical manual English produce tortuous sentences. The most obvious solution to such detouring is to use simple subject–verb–direct object construction, especially one-word verbs.

example, in the literature of data processing, words such as *parameter* and *interface* have frequently been blamed for producing prose that is difficult to read.

2. Circle all abstract verbs: all-purpose verbs that name some indefinite general action. Since this determination too is often a matter of opinion, we suggest that you count only the ones that predominate in manuals: *accomplish, affect, allow, implement, involve, perform, provide, require, support,* including past tense and passive voice.

If you find that you have circled very few words, the writing is unusually concrete. And that's good. If, on the other hand, you find that you have circled many words, then perhaps you or the experts may be victims of "abstractitis." A really acute case of this debilitating disease is marked by symptoms such as obscurity, cacophony, humbug, pedantry, and hot air.

If the writing is well into the realm of abstraction, follow the procedure explained below. It should reduce the fever and restore literary health. For our demonstration, we select the following specimen:

> The capability of performing the report printing function is provided by the 3211 printing device.

Step 1:   Cross out all abstract words like those listed above.

> ~~The capability of~~ performing the report printing ~~function~~ is provided by the 3211 printing ~~device.~~

Step 2:   Cross out all abstract verbs like those listed above and their linking words *is, was, are,* and *were.*

> ~~The capability of performing~~ the report printing ~~function is provided~~ by the 3211 printing ~~device.~~

You should now be left with *something.* There must be at least one concrete detail in a sentence if it is to have any meaning at all.

Step 3: Select one of the concrete details left and make it the subject of a new sentence, and, if possible, use the other detail as the verb. In our example, we select "report printing" as our subject and write:

| Report printing is done by the 3211.

That's better. The new version reduces fifteen words to seven. But observe that it repeats a fault described in step 2—the use of the vague (and passive) "is done." This can be corrected by making "reports" the subject:

| Reports are printed by the 3211.

It's not bad. We've cut the number of words to six. But we can do better. How? We recall the old advice: avoid the passive voice. So we try yet another revision, making "the 3211" the subject:

| The 3211 prints reports.

Now it's four words. We've taken fifteen inflated words and reduced them to four words expressing the same thought without loss of meaning or sense of dignity. Compare it with the original:

| The 3211 prints reports.   The capability of performing the
                                              report printing function is pro-
                                              vided by the 3211 printing device.

One result of this procedure is that you begin to realize how much verbiage is used to express a single thought—how much baloney can be stuffed into a single casing. What happened to the indispensable word *capability*? What happened to the beloved *function*? You begin to see that you can almost live without them and that your writing will be clearer and more direct when it is free of these empty clumps of TME.

But there's more to good writing than cutting out the abstract words. Note that the new sentence conforms to this syntactical pattern:

Subject + verb ⟶ object

That is, it conforms to Sir Arthur Quiller-Couch's wise axiom of effective writing: use transitive verbs that strike their object; and use them in the active voice, shunning the unnecessary passive with its little *is*'s and *was*'s. Writing in this way unleashes the power of verbs—the sinews of speech—and results in clearer and more readable prose. So, as a side benefit of eliminating abstract words we also relieve that other chronic ailment of TME: the passive voice.

Abstract language and the passive voice are often linked. As the number of abstract words rises, the number of active verbs drops. Stick to a vocabulary of short, specific, straightforward verbs and shun the TME vocabulary of abstract nouns and unnecessary passives.

WRITE IT THIS WAY	NOT THIS WAY
A edits B.	The editing function is performed by A.
C stamps D.	The implementation of the D stamping function is provided by C.
E dispenses F.	The capability of the F dispensing activity is provided by the E unit.

The statement "The 3211 prints reports" answers the question: What does what? If you write your material to answer this question, the chances are that you will instinctively avoid overabstraction and wordiness. You would be following these principles: What does what? Who does what? Write always with these questions in mind; write in words that stand for things you can touch and operations that you can demonstrate.

Samuel T. Williamson, an editor of *Newsweek*, once wrote: "There once was a time when everyday folk spoke one language and learned men wrote another. It was called the Dark Ages."[6] If we had only the average manual in TME to go by, we'd be forced to conclude that the Dark Ages are still with us. You and your subject-matter experts can do your part to get us out of this latter-day Dark Age.

---

[6]"How to Write Like a Social Scientist," *Saturday Review*, October 4, 1947, p. 27.

Use Plan Sheet B: What the Product or Procedure Does (Figure 2-8) to state what the product or procedure does. To explain what it does, you need to think of its purpose just as its inventor thought of it and explain the purpose using the simple subject–active verb–object formula. Figure 2-9 is an example of a filled-out Plan Sheet B.

EXPLAINING THE DISTINGUISHING CHARACTERISTICS OF THE PRODUCT OR PROCEDURE

In explaining the product or procedure's distinguishing characteristics, you and the subject-matter experts should apply two simple tests: Is the information relevant to the particular product or procedure? Is the information meaningful to your reader? To convey information that meets these two tests, we propose the following strategies:

- Be specific.
- Translate technical facts.
- Show how the product or procedure differs from similar products or procedures.
- Compare the new product or procedure with the old product or procedure.

Being Specific

A problem closely related to the overuse of abstract language, which we examined earlier in this chapter, is overgeneralization. The following passage is an all-too-frequent example of the vagueness caused by TME writing:

> The company is implementing application development activities in certain functional areas that may integrate one or more of the newer operational facilities with one or another of the older and more conventional technologies, and it is indicated that these objectives generate potential considerations that could provide the generation of product capabilities that would result in viable approaches.

PLAN SHEET B:
WHAT THE PRODUCT OR PROCEDURE DOES

To explain what a product or procedure does, you need to:

- Think about its function just as the designer thought about it
- Explain the function, using the simple subject–active verb–object formula

Name of product or procedure	+	Active functional verb	+	Object of action

Fig. 2-8   Plan Sheet B: What the Product or Procedure Does.

PLAN SHEET B:
WHAT THE PRODUCT OR PROCEDURE DOES

To explain what a product or procedure does, you need to:

- Think about its function just as the designer thought about it
- Explain the function, using the simple subject–active verb–object formula

Name of product or procedure	+	Active functional verb	+	Object of action
Escalator	+	Moves	+	Passengers up and down between floors
Lens	+	Converges or diverges	+	Light rays
Afterburner	+	Augments	+	Thrust of a jet engine by burning additional fuel with the uncombined oxygen in the exhaust gas
Laser	+	Amplifies	+	Visible, ultraviolet, and infrared light
Compass	+	Draws	+	Circles or arcs
Compass	+	Determines	+	Geographical direction

Fig. 2-9 Example of filled-out Plan Sheet B.

Your first reaction might be that the sentence is too long and should be split into two separate ones. That's a good idea. Let's see if that helps.

> The company is implementing application development activities in certain functional areas that may integrate one or more of the newer operational facilities with one or another of the older and more conventional technologies. It is indicated that these objectives generate potential consideration that could provide the generation of product capabilities that would result in viable approaches.

Do you understand what the passage means? Do you think anybody understands what it means? What reader can struggle through the TME phrases? The point is that the passage *can* be translated into almost any statement about any business. That's what happens when TME phrases such as "implementing application development activities," "functional areas," "newer operational facilities," and "generate potential considerations" take over. Try translating the sentences into a specific statement about a business that makes paper pulp, or refines petroleum, or distills alcoholic beverages, or manufactures pharmaceuticals, or smelts zinc, or. . . .

How the product differs from similar products is sometimes important to the reader's understanding of what is to follow in a manual. In stating the distinguishing characteristics, you should be so specific that the reader can read your words and fill in the blank space where the name of the product or procedure goes. After reading the following definition, fill in the blank.

> _____ is a thick-set, mostly very large, nearly hairless four-footed mammal having the snout prolonged into a muscular trunk and two incisors in the upper jaw developed especially in the male into long tusks which furnish ivory.

If the reader can't fill in the blank with the correct word or words, then the passage is too general. The above passage may not be a literary masterpiece, but the reader can fill in the blank with the correct name.

What it means to overgeneralize is made even clearer by comparison of the following two passages.

SAMPLE A

The typing requirements of modern management vary widely even within a single company; _____*_____ meets this challenge with the most complete line of typewriters available from a single source, designed to fulfill every typing requirement from the president's correspondence to the mailroom's labels. Each _____*_____ typewriter is intended for specific purposes; to each of these it brings speed, ease of operation, and dependability.

*In these slots, you could put the name of any typewriter manufacturer since the invention of the typewriter in 1867, and the name would fit. When you can substitute anything for the subject of a paragraph, it really says nothing. *That's* overgeneralization.

SAMPLE B

A typewriter that uses no ribbon? That has no typebars, no typing ball? After 13 years of research and development, the _____**_____ typewriter is here. You type as usual, but the letters are formed or erased by *laser*. Result: the best-looking copy you've ever seen. Advantages: you can adjust the height of letters, individually or by word. And no typebars or ball means absolutely *quiet* typing.

**In this slot, only one name fits: the Lasermatic 203. When only one name fits as the subject of a paragraph, it says something. It's informative; it's specific; it has meaning.

Translating Technical Facts

At some time you probably have been told to "skip the rhetoric and give just the facts." That advice is fine when you are talking with persons who know the subject well and want only a condensed statement of the technical data. (And—we might add—when those persons are able to ask questions about the data.) However, there are times when you should translate technical data: when you reasonably believe your readers won't be able to understand the significance of the technical data, and when you don't know how much your readers know about the subject. The first situation presents no problem. For example, telling a reader who doesn't know much about stereo equipment that the Jazzum 60A 2-way bass-reflex speakers have 8-inch core woofers, core tweeters with a frequency range of 50 to 20,000 hertz with maximum output of 20 watts won't help the reader understand its distinguishing characteristics. You know you're playing verbal solitaire. You've cut out the reader.

The second situation doesn't present as big a problem as most people think. Contrary to popular belief, most intelligent readers are not insulted by being told something they already know. They are inwardly pleased to have their knowledge confirmed. While we are not suggesting that you tell the knowledgeable reader what the technical data means, we are suggesting that when you can't be sure that the meaning is clear you should spell it out. The fear of offending intelligent readers by underrating their knowledge is pretty much groundless.

Heed the warning of the wise editor who said: "Don't forget that your reader is silently interrupting you every ten lines to ask, 'Why?' 'What for?' or 'Well, what of it?' " and if you don't answer these questions the reader will soon stop reading.

If you write with those questions in mind, you won't be playing verbal solitaire. In other words, it is not enough to merely list technical facts about the product. You must translate those facts so that they become meaningful to your readers. So deal your readers in. Remember, most of them are first-time users of the product or procedure you write about. As Figure 2-10 shows, by providing the "so what?" you make what you say have some value to your reader.

Translating technical facts may appear to work against brevity. It does in one way: it adds words to your text. But being brief can mean being unintelligible to readers who don't know what the technical facts mean. If it takes more words to make it easier for your readers, use them.

Plan Sheet C: Translating Technical Facts (Figure 2-11) is a simple two-column format that will aid you in translating technical facts. The left-hand column presents the facts; the right-hand column explains how the reader benefits from (or is otherwise affected by) them. Figure 2-12 shows a filled-out Plan Sheet C.

Showing How the Product Differs from Similar Products or Procedures

Plan Sheet D: The Distinguishing Characteristics of the Product or Procedure (Figure 2-13) is a template to guide you and the subject-matter experts in writing specific and informative statements about

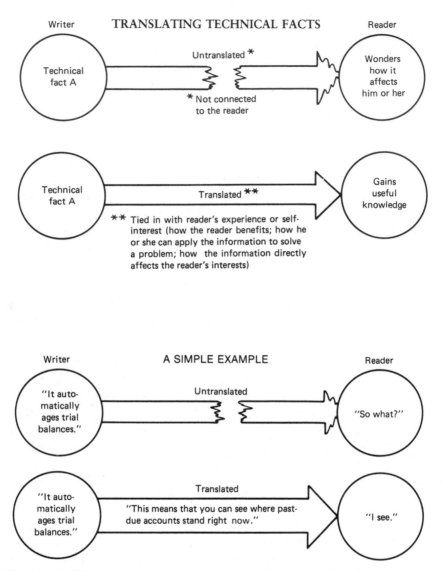

Fig. 2-10 William James, the noted American philosopher and psychologist of the late nineteenth and early twentieth centuries, wrote that facts are stupid things by themselves and are meaningful only when attached to an idea. Be sure that the facts in your manual mean something to your readers.

PLAN SHEET C:
TRANSLATING TECHNICAL FACTS

The fact	The significance

Fig. 2-11 Plan Sheet C: Translating Technical Facts.

PLAN SHEET C:
TRANSLATING TECHNICAL FACTS

The fact	The significance
Our best bookend because of these important reasons:	
• Solid tubular steel	All corners are rounded; no sharp edges to cut your hand or tear your book jackets
• Chrome-plated	Won't rust
• Friction-fit	Won't slide; stays in place; holds more firmly

Fig. 2-12 Example of filled-out Plan Sheet C.

PLAN SHEET D:
THE DISTINGUISHING CHARACTERISTICS OF THE PRODUCT OR PROCEDURE

1. Use details.

2. Use illustrations.

3. Use comparisons and contrasts.

   Answer questions such as: Why is it better? How does it differ from older equipment, methods, procedures, products? What is it like? What is it unlike? What does it look like? What does it work like?

4. Use analogies.

5. Use analysis.

6. Use definitions.

   • Definition by illustration

   • Definition by comparison or contrast

   • Definition by analysis (defining a product or procedure by placing it in a general class and then explaining how it differs from other members of the same class)

The term	Its general class	How it differs

   • Definition by history (defining the product or procedure by showing the changes in meaning it has taken on over a long period of time)

Fig. 2-13 Plan Sheet D: The Distinguishing Characteristics of the Product or Procedure

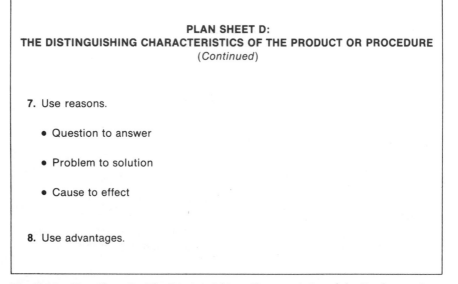

Fig. 2-13   Plan Sheet D: The Distinguishing Characteristics of the Product or Procedure (*Continued*).

the product, and to help you avoid meaningless generalities. As you use the template, remember to look for places where you should translate technical information into meaningful statements. Plan Sheet D identifies eight ways to generate information that meets the test of relevance. You won't always be able to apply all the ways to every product or procedure. Some will be more relevant than others. But merely by using some of the ways, you will be able to get enough ideas to begin your writing. Figure 2-14 shows a filled-out Plan Sheet D.

Comparing the Old and the New

The cumulative nature of technological changes means that product and procedural innovations build upon earlier products and procedures. Thus, almost any new product or procedure can be related to those that it replaces. However, seldom is the reader helped in bridging from the old to the new; more often he or she must figure out alone how the new relates to the old. It's as if the new enjoyed no legacy from the past.

Plan Sheet E: The Old Product or Procedure (Figure 2-15) shows what the *old* product or procedure looks like. If it's a product, it is described part by part; if it's a process, step by step. Plan Sheet F: The New Product or Procedure (Figure 2-16) shows what the *new* product or procedure looks like—part by part or step by step. Figure 2-17 is an example of a filled-out Plan Sheet E. Figure 2-18 shows a filled-out Plan Sheet F.

If possible, lay out the manual so that Plan Sheet E will be a left-hand page and Plan Sheet F will be a right-hand page. They should face each other for easy comparison.

Here is the key point: *there must be a direct visual comparison* between what is shown in a strip of Plan Sheet E and what is shown in a strip of Plan Sheet F. It is almost impossible to overemphasize the importance of visual communication, whether you're referring to photographs or line drawings or to graphs and charts.

Under the heading "Commentary" on Plan Sheet F, the subject-matter experts add the words to support and reinforce what the reader is seeing. Remember—nothing is self-explanatory, not even a picture. The commentary may be arranged in several different ways: by order of importance, space, or chronology, or in any way that is logically or psychologically significant to the reader.

USING THE FILLED-OUT PLAN SHEETS A TO F

"That writer does the most," goes an adage attributed to at least a half-dozen authors, "who gives the reader the most knowledge, and takes from the reader the least time." Many manuals read as though the writers wished to give their readers the least knowledge and take from them the most time.

In our discussion of how to explain what the product or procedure is, we've tried to show a few things you can do about the problem. Plan Sheets A to F now give you what you need to reach your reader—relevant information about the product or procedure, not overly technical data that you would be forced to translate (if you could). And although these plan sheets are pretty much in the form

PLAN SHEET D:
THE DISTINGUISHING CHARACTERISTICS OF THE PRODUCT OR PROCEDURE

1. Use details.

   Machine X is versatile. It has a continuous band. . . . It cuts. . . . It also. . . .

2. Use illustrations.

   Machine X is versatile. A large midwestern distributor computes its . . . and . . . . With machine X. . . .

3. Use comparisons and contrasts.

   Answer questions such as: Why is it better? How does it differ from older equipment, methods, procedures, products? What is it like? What is it unlike? What does it look like? What does it work like?

   The principal difference between Jupiter A and Jupiter B is that. . . .

   Like machine X, machine Y converts. . . . Like machine X, it cuts. . . . Unlike machine X, machine Y cannot. . . .

4. Use analogies.

   Programming this machine is like playing chess. . . . You have the same . . ., the same. . . .

   It's like the tab key on a typewriter. It lets you skip over fields you don't want. . . .

5. Use analysis.

   The two main types of welding are (1) x-ing and (2) y-ing. In x-ing, all joints are . . . and. . . . In y-ing, only the . . . are. . . .

6. Use definitions.

   • Definition by illustration
   Program X is best for companies with less than 150 employees. For example, Company A, which has used Program X for three years, reports that. . . . Company B. . . .

   • Definition by comparison or contrast
   Like machine X, machine Y has four stackers. But unlike machine X, it does not sort. . . .

Fig. 2-14   Example of a filled-out Plan Sheet D.

PLAN SHEET D:
THE DISTINGUISHING CHARACTERISTICS OF THE PRODUCT OR PROCEDURE
(Continued)

- Definition by analysis (defining a product or procedure by placing it in a general class and then explaining how it differs from other members of the same class)

The term	Its general class	How it differs
A widget	is a printer	that works by ultra-violet radiation
A gramble	is a sales report	that shows sales according to moon phases

- Definition by history (defining the product or procedure by showing the changes in meaning it has taken on over a long period of time)

A gronkle was once the most widely used machine for measuring. . . . But early in the 1970s, the influence of. . . .

7. Use reasons.

- Question to answer

Why would a gronkle print reports faster even though it has a slower gravitor? First, it. . . .

- Problem to solution

Company B's decision to install a gronkle led to a crisis. . . . The 75K machine seems to be the only answer, because. . . .

- Cause to effect

If you don't use a power drill to make the hole, you might face a serious problem in. . . . First, you. . . . Second, you. . . .

8. Use advantages.

It automatically controls four widgets at the same time. This means that you no longer have to. . . .

X is especially useful when you want to . . . or when you have to. . . .

As a _____ for _____, the X product offers you several advantages:

1. (Time)
2. (Effort)
3. (Speed)

4. (Accuracy)
5. (Ease of operation)
6. (And so on)

```
┌─────────────────────────────────────────────────────────┐
│                                                         │
│                    PLAN SHEET E:                        │
│              THE OLD PRODUCT OR PROCEDURE               │
│                                                         │
│                                                         │
│   Title of product or procedure _____     │
│                                                         │
├─────────────────────────────────────────────────────────┤
│                                                         │
│                                                         │
│                                                         │
│                                                         │
│                                                         │
│                                                         │
│                                                         │
├─────────────────────────────────────────────────────────┤
│                                                         │
│                                                         │
│                                                         │
│                                                         │
│                                                         │
│                                                         │
├─────────────────────────────────────────────────────────┤
│                                                         │
│                                                         │
│                                                         │
│                                                         │
│                                                         │
│                                                         │
└─────────────────────────────────────────────────────────┘
```

Fig. 2-15 Plan Sheet E: The Old Product or Procedure. Illustrating the old way.

PLAN SHEET F:
THE NEW PRODUCT OR PROCEDURE

Title of product or procedure _____

Commentary

Commentary

Commentary

Fig. 2-16   Plan Sheet F: The New Product or Procedure. Illustrating the new way.

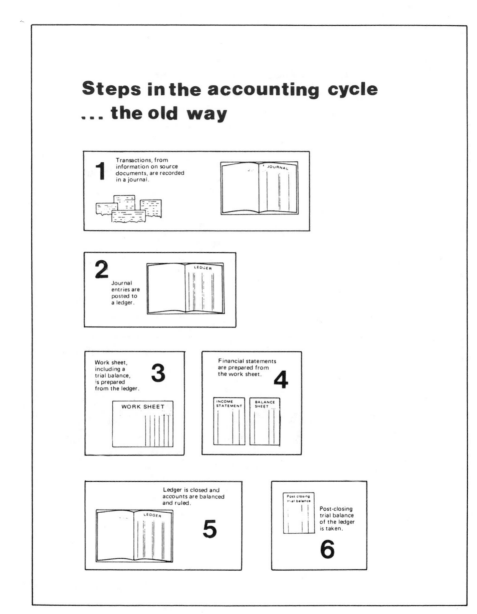

Fig. 2-17   Example of filled-out Plan Sheet E.

Fig. 2-18 Example of filled-out Plan Sheet F. (*Courtesy of International Business Machines Corporation*)

that you would use in the finished manual, they can be enhanced by a graphics expert.

With this relevant information you will not be tempted to dream up one of those stereotyped, overly general, vague, uninformative introductions that waste your reader's time. You can now organize the beginning of your manual to give your grateful reader a firm handle on the information that follows.

THREE

Explaining How to Use the Product or Procedure

Although we have already discussed naming the product or procedure, explaining its purpose, and describing its distinguishing characteristics—information that goes into the introduction of the manual—we suggest that you write the introduction *last*. Before you write your introduction, first put down step by step what your reader must do to perform the job.

Concentrate all your energy and thinking into getting the procedural part—the most important part—of your manual complete and accurate. After the procedural part of your manual is done, and only then, go back and write a brief introduction. Brief.

Why write the manual in what seems to be a backward fashion? Because once you get the procedural part done—the foundation in place—you can then build a better introduction, one with some *useful* information in it.

Writers who start out by spending a lot of time straining over an introduction waste their time on what is really a secondary (although an important) part of the manual. They try for profound thoughts, profoundly expressed. And the result is usually not worth the effort. So don't confuse the *writing* sequence with the information gathering, the reporting, or the reading sequence. Just because the reader reads the introduction first doesn't mean that you should actually write the introduction first.

What is so lacking in the procedural part of most manuals is an organized, step-by-step set of clear and straightforward instructions for accomplishing a task.

Look at the procedural part of almost any manual. Often, the information is crowded into a paragraph of traditional narrative form. Often, a specific instruction is buried in the middle of a paragraph of general description. Often, the instructions are phrased in descriptive, not instructional, language. Often, in the list of instructions there are tremendous logic jumps. Often, too, there are not enough graphics.

The results are predictable. Readers using manuals with inappropriate format and style and no graphics take longer to perform the work and make more errors than those using manuals with appropriate format, style, and graphics. Readers using manuals that omit necessary information or contain a great deal of extraneous material cannot or will not continue to follow the text.

This chapter discusses the use of three plan sheets to help you complete the procedural part of the manual:

- Plan Sheet G: The Task Outline Sheet is a flowchart of the process the reader must follow from start to finish.
- Plan Sheet H: The Task Detail Sheet details each block in the flowchart, breaking it into the specific steps the reader is to take in performing the work.
- Plan Sheet I: The Alternatives Sheet explains alternative courses of action the reader may decide to take.

As you work through these plan sheets, concentrate on getting the information your reader will need to do the job successfully. Nothing less, nothing more.

OUTLINING THE TASK

Plan Sheet G: The Task Outline Sheet (see Figure 3-1) talks a language familiar to the subject-matter expert: flowcharting. Since each job will be different, we do not provide a blank Plan Sheet G. You and the subject-matter experts should create your own by listing each step in the order in which it occurs in the job procedure. Then visu-

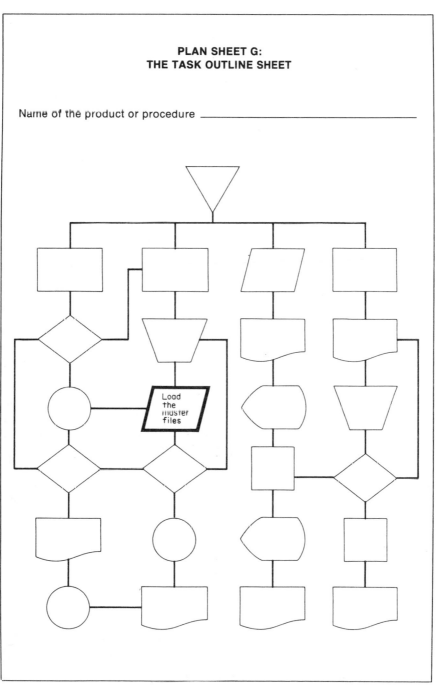

Fig. 3-1 Example of the task outline sheet used as a control tool.

alize the list by converting it into a block diagram or similar flow-chart. Begin the name of each step with an imperative verb, for example, "Load the master files." This should be an easy task for the subject-matter experts. Together with them, you create a flowchart of the procedure the reader must follow from start to finish to do the work.

Filled out, the task outline sheet serves two important purposes. You can:

1. Use it strictly as a control tool for keeping the manual on track for everyone concerned with producing the manual, as in Figure 3-1, or

2. Convert it into a different, simplified graphic more understand-able to the reader, as in Figure 3-2, in which it serves as a graphic overview for major stages of the procedure covered by the manual.

However, the task outline sheet serves primarily as a tool for filling out the next form, Plan Sheet H: The Task Detail Sheet (see Figures 3-3 and 3-4), which gives the detailed breakdown of the task, step by step. Note the block in the task outline sheet (Figure 3-1) stating "Load the master files." Turn to the filled-out task detail sheet (Figure 3-5) and note that the task reads "Load the master files." For every block in the flowchart of the task outline sheet, there is a detailed breakdown of that task in the task detail sheet. Thus, the task outline sheet is a prerequisite for the task detail sheet.

The discipline of completing the task outline sheet will help everybody concerned: the subject-matter experts, because they will have to organize their thoughts in a logical manner; you, the writer, because you will have a road map to the organization of the manual; the artists, because they will have a better idea of what's needed.

Comprehensive, Logical, and Relevant Flowcharts

What we often find in manuals, if we compare them to recipes, is that only the ingredients are listed. So, if the manual is about how to drive a car, it may list the necessary parts: an ignition key, a gear shift, a

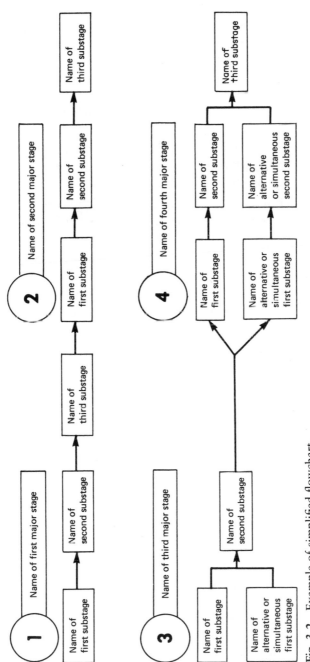

Fig. 3-2 Example of simplified flowchart.

clutch, a gas pedal, a brake pedal, etc. But how the reader puts things together and in what sequence—while included in well-written recipes—is often missing in manuals. Therefore the whole energy and effort in learning what to do, how to get started, and what to do next is thrust completely upon the reader.

Tell the reader what to do first, how to get started, what to do next, and so forth. The flowchart is important because when things are set down in a segmented visual pattern, it is both easier to comprehend the process portrayed and to perceive its flaws. The flowchart is a skeletal outline of the manual, the blueprint we spoke of in the introduction to this book.

The first step in creating the flowchart for the task outline sheet is to have the subject-matter experts list all the tasks that the reader may have to perform and then draw the entire procedure from beginning to end. The subject-matter experts will have to do it, because nobody else will know the procedure as well as they do. If the purpose of the manual is to explain how to drive a car, the outline should begin with opening the door to get in and end with turning off the ignition, setting the brake, and getting out of the car. It must be sequential.

The second step is to control the quality of the flowchart by simulation of the process. Verifying the flowchart is the only way to make sure that the subject-matter experts are giving you an accurate blueprint. Here's where you must represent the reader well by trying to follow the instructions in their skeletal form as they are shown on the flowchart. And, in effect, at this point, not only will you be working with the organization of the procedural part of the manual, you will also be testing for feasibility—verifying the procedure with the technical staff, the subject-matter experts. If at any point there is confusion, you know that you've found a weak point. You know that something is out of order or is missing or is poorly stated.

Consider this for a moment: The product was designed for the reader (consumer), but the manual at this stage may *not* be designed for him or her. You must simulate the reader's situation to check whether he or she will be able to carry out the instructions embodied in the flowchart. In your simulation, you'll be checking the flowchart against three criteria—comprehensiveness, logic, and relevance.

1. Are all the discrete steps present in the procedure? That is, is the flowchart *comprehensive*?

A common fault in many manuals is the omission of information that the reader needs. Common sense, of course, tells us to write to the reader's knowledge and experience. However, common sense often is not strong enough to overcome the subject-matter experts' tendency to forget how much they have learned about the procedure and their assumption that "everybody knows this." Such oversight leads to instructions that tell the reader how to perform a particular task on a unit but fail to tell the reader how to find the unit (to change the windshield wiper motor, the reader must know where it is located) or what to do with residuals (how to dispose of five quarts of old oil, for instance). Keep checking until you are sure there is no missing information or logical gaps to confuse the reader.

2. Are all the steps in the right order? That is, is the flowchart *logical*?

There may be some latitude here. Sometimes it makes little difference if the order is changed (for instance, cutting off the ignition, putting the gear in park, and setting the emergency brake is just as good as putting the gear in park, setting the emergency brake, and cutting off the ignition). Or there may be alternative sequences, depending upon certain contingencies, that will force a change in the order of the action. But give the reader at least one good way to go. Later, if the reader wants to experiment with the sequence, he or she may do so. But at least give the reader one simple, reliable way to do the job.

3. Does the flowchart include only information needed to do the work? That is, are all parts of the flowchart *relevant*?

Here the problem is the opposite of omitted information: information is included that is of no help to the reader in performing the task. Remember that the subject-matter experts see a much larger set of connections than the reader often needs. Some subject-matter experts, in their zeal to be comprehensive, never seem to be satisfied that they have explained enough, and they often include unnecessary information. They become infatuated with the complexities of the technology and lose sight of the reader, forgetting that others aren't as interested in the technicalities of the subject as they are. As a result, irrelevant information will likely appear in the manual unless you have a way to screen it.

The reader is not supposed to understand everything that interests the subject-matter experts. The reader has to understand only that part of the real world that he or she is going to have to deal with. Including irrelevant information in a manual is almost as bad as including misinformation.

What we are talking about is *scope*—restricting the manual to what the reader needs to know to do the job. It's fine for the reader to want to progress further and learn more about the product or procedure, but that's the mission of a different document. If you write to inform a pilot how to carry out a certain maneuver, for example, you don't need to describe the aileron manufacturing process. Remember that the manual should be job-oriented and reader-oriented, not design-oriented or engineer-oriented.

The test here is *what does the reader need to know to do the job?* Audience analysis is the key. A maintenance worker needs something different from the accountant or the office worker who operates the machine. The weekend hobbyist needs something different from the professional mechanic. But very often we have in one document different kinds of information suitable for different audiences. And that shows poor judgment, because the executive is interested in something quite different from what interests the machine operator who has to press the buttons to get the payroll checks out. Executives are interested in the fact that the payroll is going out in about 2 hours when it used to take 2 days. Operators need to know how to get the payroll out in those 2 hours. Maintenance workers are not interested in getting the payroll out—they're interested in learning how to get the machine going again in case it fails. So we need to design manuals for specific purposes for specific readers. Therefore, specific job-oriented blueprints must be drawn.

Once the task outline sheet is complete, you have the major procedural steps of your manual outlined. As stated before, there are several approaches you may take with this plan sheet. It can be a tool, or it can serve as a foundation for the type of approach shown in Figure 3-2, which gives the reader a graphic overview of the manual or a section of the manual.

Simplifying Flowcharts

As a control to ensure that the subject-matter experts chart the activity comprehensively and logically, the task outline sheet works well. But in order for the reader to use it as a tool, it will most likely have to be simplified.

You can simplify flowcharts by establishing a hierarchy of major stages for the procedure and subordinating the individual steps under the appropriate major stages. It's fairly easy to do, and it will have the effect of communicating to the reader the substance of the task outline sheet.

Of all the obstacles the mind must overcome when learning new information, the most important is probably the limited capacity to receive and recall information. Building upon the mathematical theory of information developed by communication theorists in the early 1950s, psychologists and educators began to view humans as processors of information who struggle to impose organization on the information they receive. The theory has implications for us. To overcome the reader's finite limits to recall, we must make him or her aware of the organizational structures of our information. We also must limit the pieces of information that we want the reader to remember at any one time.

As an example of how unrevealed organizational structure and the sheer weight of numbers adversely affect readers, let's consider a publication one of us worked on recently. The publication described a firm's annual business planning cycle, for which the author had included an astonishingly complicated flowchart to depict the firm's management-by-objectives procedures. The subject-matter expert had divided the procedure into forty-four steps. The result was a three-page foldout of an almost unreadable thicket of geometric shapes, lines, and static description. To the reader the flowchart would have been an impenetrable maze. The solution was fairly simple—using a hierarchical structure to group the forty-four steps into five major stages so the reader would regard the procedure as having five major stages, not forty-four. We believe it is inconvenient, perhaps downright misleading, not to use hierarchies to reveal organizational patterns of this kind for complex procedures. Figure 3-2 shows how to reduce an eleven-step procedure to four major stages by nesting steps under major stages.

DETAILING THE TASK

Plan Sheet G: The Task Outline Sheet identified the major procedural tasks to be covered in the manual. In Plan Sheet H: The Task Detail Sheet (Figures 3-3 and 3-4), the subject-matter experts identify each task and state it in terms of performance. Then they list the equipment and supplies needed to perform the task. Finally they break down the task into specific, clearly stated instructions, step by step, which are numbered so that there is no confusion as to what the reader does first, second, third, and so on. The tabular format of the task detail sheet encourages you to arrange your information in the order and format you will use when writing the manual. Figures 3-5 and 3-6 are examples of a filled-out task detail sheet.

Identifying the Task and Stating the Performance Objective

On the first page of the task detail sheet the subject-matter experts state the task exactly as in the corresponding block from the task outline sheet. For example, "Load the master files."

Then they state the task in the form of a performance objective:

> Given diskettes Z1200, Z1300, Z1800, a 3110 computer with 8.6 megabytes, and at least one printer, the reader will be able to load customer master records into the master file at the rate of twenty per hour, with no more than one error every forty records.

Or,

> Using capillary tubes (heparinized, if nonclotted blood is needed), gauze or cotton and alcohol, a sterile lancet, and a small test tube, the reader

PLAN SHEET H:
THE TASK DETAIL SHEET (*first page*)

Task: _____

_____

Performance objective: _____

_____

_____

_____

_____

Equipment: _____

_____

_____

_____

_____

_____

_____

Supplies: _____

_____

_____

_____

_____

_____

Fig. 3-3 Plan Sheet H: The Task Detail Sheet (first page).

PLAN SHEET H:
THE TASK DETAIL SHEET (*subsequent page*)

Step	Instruction	Supporting graphics	Notes

Fig. 3-4   Plan Sheet H: The Task Detail Sheet (subsequent page).

PLAN SHEET H:
THE TASK DETAIL SHEET (*first page*)

Task: Load the master files.

Performance objective: Given diskettes Z1200, Z1300, Z1800, a 3110 computer with 8.6 megabytes, and at least one printer, the reader will be able to load customer master records into the master file at the rate of twenty per hour, with no more than one error every forty records.

Equipment: See above.

Supplies: See above.

Fig. 3-5   Example of filled-out Plan Sheet H (first page).

PLAN SHEET H:
THE TASK DETAIL SHEET (*subsequent page*)

Step	Instruction	Supporting graphics	Notes
1	Assign a unique account number to each customer.	An explanation of three alternative methods with their advantages and disadvantages, plus examples.	
2	Fill out a DX-09.	Illustration of a filled-out DX-09 form.	
3	Back up the master files by running RVBACKUP . . .

and so on. | Illustration of the procedure. | |

Fig. 3-6   Example of filled-out Plan Sheet H (subsequent page).

will be able to perform a capillary puncture and draw capillary blood within 90 seconds.

If the objective cannot be met by a person representative of the intended audience, then it is set unreasonably high or the instructions are vague. Later, you will want to test everything for clarity and comprehensiveness, but you can impose two controls at this stage: write your performance objectives according to the method described subsequently, and work hard at making your vocabulary clear.

In writing the performance objectives, keep in mind the principles of stating them clearly and meaningfully while you and the subject-matter experts write and rewrite them. Performance objectives should be very concrete and specific. Avoid abstract concepts such as bravery, agility, knowledge, or performance, describing only the concrete and specific behavior (or performance) regarded as evidence of them. For instance, a youngster doesn't say "Hey, watch me demonstrate my balance and muscular coordination," but something like "Hey, watch me walk this old fence." He or she is thinking in terms of performance, not abstraction. Performance objectives must be this concrete.

Mager's *Preparing Instructional Objectives* is extremely helpful with its clear statement of these principles. Mager recommends the following method, which we have adapted for manual writing.

1. Identify the desired performance by name; you can specify the kind of reader performance that will be accepted as evidence that a given part of the manual has achieved its objective.

2. Define the desired performance further by describing the important conditions under which the performance will be expected to occur.

3. Specify the criteria of acceptable performance by describing how well the reader must do the job.

Let's look at a couple of objectives. First, state the desired performance by name:

The reader will be able to enter the orders and print out invoices for them.

Or,

> The reader will be able to replace the upper radiator hose on a passenger automobile.

Second, state the conditions you will impose on the reader when he or she is demonstrating mastery of the objective:

> *Given diskette Z109A, a 3110 computer, and twenty customer orders,* the reader will be able to enter orders and print out invoices.

Or,

> *Given a standard set of tools,* the reader will be able to replace the upper radiator hose in a passenger automobile.

Third, state how you will recognize success:

> Given diskette Z109A, a 3110 computer, and twenty customer orders, the reader will be able to enter orders and print out invoices for them *within 25 minutes. Only one error is allowed.*

Or,

> Given a standard set of tools, the reader will be able to replace the upper radiator hose in a passenger automobile *in 25 minutes.*

To test a statement of objectives for clarity and completeness, evaluate in terms of these three major features:

1. Does the statement describe what the reader will be *doing* to demonstrate that he or she has reached the objective?
2. Does the statement describe the important conditions (givens or restrictions, or both) under which the reader will be expected to demonstrate competence?

3. Does the statement indicate how the reader will be evaluated? Does it describe at least the lower limits of acceptable performance?

The second control is to work at making your vocabulary clear. Take, for example, the word *heparinized* in one of the earlier objectives. It is a legitimate technical term that the reader will have to learn. Therefore, part of your task as writer is to increase your reader's technical vocabulary. But don't use TME, and when you use legitimate technical terminology, define it. Don't send the reader to a dictionary or other reference.

Listing Equipment and Supplies

Some of the sample performance objectives in the preceding section identified the equipment (hardware, tools, etc.) and supplies (items consumed during the procedure—gauze, cotton, upper radiator hose, etc.) required in performing the task. But since the performance objective may not be defined that precisely in the set of instructions or since the list of equipment and supplies may be lengthy, you need to provide the reader with a list of items needed. In making the list, always strive for the absolute clarity that you strive for in other parts of the manual. This is not a place to allow (or force) the reader to interpret (or guess) what is needed.

Lay out the equipment and supplies section like a checklist. Be specific. Be motivational. If a funnel is needed to pour coolant into a radiator, explain that it is needed and what size funnel will work best. If a *gallon* of *liquid* cleanser is required, say so; don't tell the reader to get an "adequate amount of cleaner." Explain what the equipment or supplies are to be used for. If a wire brush is to be used to clean a metal coupler, say so. Such precise explanations of what is needed, and why, help overcome any possible negative response of the reader, such as "it doesn't seem reasonable to have to get this."

A checklist of equipment and supplies required to install a ceramic tile floor is illustrated in Figure 3-7. Be that specific. You and the subject-matter experts obviously know what is needed to perform the procedure. Don't count on your readers knowing unless you tell them.

EQUIPMENT AND SUPPLIES

- A glass cutter for scoring the tiles.

- A commercial tile cutter for cutting straight edges in the tile. Tile dealers have tile cutters to rent. Some will even lend tile cutters when you purchase your tile from them. Ask for operating instructions from the tile dealer.

- Tile nippers for cutting notches in the tile.

- A sanding block with 50- or 60-grit aluminum oxide–coated sandpaper for smoothing the cut edges of the tile.

- A notched trowel for applying the adhesive to the back of the tiles.

- A rubber-surfaced trowel for applying grout between the tiles.

- A damp sponge for removing excess grout from the surface of the tiles and for cleaning the tiles with muriatic acid.

- Rubber gloves for protecting hands when cleaning with muriatic acid.

- Spacers for uniformly separating all the tiles.*

- Adhesive to apply to back of the tiles.*

- Grout for filling in between the tiles.*

- Muriatic acid for cleaning tiles after grout has dried.*

* See Section 1 for instructions on how to estimate the area of floor to be covered. Take the dimensions on a sketch to the tile dealer to help determine the number of tiles and spacers needed and the amount of adhesive, grout, and muriatic acid needed. Mix grout according to manufacturer's instructions. Mix a solution of 1 part muriatic acid and 10 parts water.

Fig. 3-7   Sample list of equipment and supplies needed to perform a procedure.

Dividing the Task into Steps

On the second and subsequent pages of the task detail sheet are four columns for:

- Numbering the steps of the procedure
- Writing the instructions
- Making notations about supporting graphics
- Making notes about warnings, cautions, and contingencies

Numbering the Steps of the Procedure. Numbering each step helps the reader find his or her place when looking back and forth between the manual and the work. It also aids the reader in following references to steps performed previously or to steps later in the procedure. You should also consider putting check boxes in front of the numbers to make the instructions into a check-off worksheet. Sectioning of instructions is useful when there are many steps that may be subordinated under major stages, but the numbers should run consecutively through all sections.

Writing the Instructions. Since you are now writing the how-to section, major parts of it will be devoted to giving instructions. Remember that the word *instruction* best expresses the main reason for writing and publishing the manual. Make sure your instructions read like instructions, not descriptions or suggestions (see Figure 3-8). To attain that aim, impose three disciplines.

First, *begin every instruction with a specific imperative verb.* This injunction ensures that you do not write instructions in descriptive or vague language. It also ensures that you do not phrase instructions in the passive voice, one of the worst problems in manuals. It also ensures that you do not conspicuously overuse conditional statements and emphatic *must*s. More importantly, it ensures that the TME verbs *to provide, to perform the X function,* and *to accomplish X* do not creep in. The following statements show how inappropriate style raises questions about the intent of the statements and the relationship between the writer and reader. Is what follows instructional, descriptive, suggestive, or what?

1. A piece of paper is used.
2. A pencil is picked up.
3. A circle should be drawn in the upper half of the paper.
4. A square may be drawn in the lower half.
5. A dot may be put in the middle of the circle.
6. An X may be provided in the square.
7. A line should be drawn to provide the connection between the dot and the X.

Do you feel strongly directed by such language? If this was intended to be a set of instructions, it would probably not get the job done. To tell the reader *how to* do something—which is the main purpose of the procedural part of the manual—use instructional language, and

Instructional	Semi-instructional	Descriptive	TME jargon
Reserve numbers 999 to 1999 for new accounts.	Numbers 999 to 1999 should be reserved for new accounts.	Numbers 999 to 1999 are reserved for new accounts.	Implementation of the account numbering function is provided by the reservation of numbers 999 to 1999 for the new account area.
Built on a specific direct verb of command, here *reserve*, which usually begins the sentence.	Verb becomes passive, usually coupled with *should be, may be, can be, must be, will be, shall be,* and the like.	Verb becomes passive, coupled with *is, are, was, were, will be, has been, have been,* and so on.	Real verb disappears, transformed into some other part of speech (a noun or an adjective). A "false" verb replaces it: *is provided, is performed, is supported,* and others.

The finishing touch: an injection of stereotyped pseudo-technical words—*implementation, capability, function, concept, facility, support, parameter,* and the like. |

Fig. 3-8   Description is not instruction. To tell your reader *how to* do something—which is the main purpose of the manual—use *instructional* language, not semi-instructional language, not descriptive language, and certainly not TME jargon.

certainly not TME jargon. The test here is fairly simple. Just ask yourself whether the reader is likely to grasp at once the instructional nature of the statement.

Second, *use conditional statements only for stating desired results.* Don't write *should be, may be,* and other forms that are more appropriate to suggestions. For example, note in Figure 3-9 that the sen-

Wrong	Right
Procedure for laying out a building	*Procedure for laying out a building*
1. The corners of the building should be squared.	1. Square the corners of the building.
2. Stakes *A, B, C,* and *D* may be driven 4 to 10 feet from *a, b, c,* and *d,* respectively.	2. Drive stakes *A, B, C,* and *D* 4 to 10 feet from *a, b, c,* and *d,* respectively.
3. Batter boards to *A, B, C,* and *D* should be erected. A hosed funnel may be used to get the same elevation for all batter boards.	3. Erect batter boards to *A, B, C,* and *D.* Use a hosed funnel to get the same elevation for all batter boards.
4. Building lines should be strung to pass directly over *a, b, c,* and *d* (a plumb line should be used) and should be tied to the batter boards.	4. String building lines to pass directly over *a, b, c,* and *d* (use a plumb line) and tie to the batter boards.
5. The foundation and excavation lines may be established from the building lines.	5. Establish the foundation and excavation lines from the building lines.

Fig. 3-9   Use imperative, not conditional, statements (use conditional statements only for stating desired results).

tences on the right *tell* the reader to do something; those on the left don't. Note also that the sentences on the right are at least 20 percent shorter than those on the left. Thus, by this very simple step, you reduce the length of major parts of the manual by a fifth. And that's not bad.

The misuse of *should* may also cause confusion, as illustrated in the passages in Figure 3-10. *Should,* as used in the first and third sentences in the left-hand passage, implies an option where none actually exists: unless the reader does those actions, he or she cannot balance the accounts. Save *should* for stating desirable results or conditions, as in the following statements:

The air pressure gauge should read 38 pounds per square inch.

If you are 6 feet tall, you should weigh. . . .

Make a running lace of ten ties along the dowel. There should be a tie approximately each ½ inch.

Original	Rewritten
The totals printed for Accounts Receivable and Collections on the register *should be recorded* on the appropriate line of the Audit Control log. The beginning balance on the register *should be equal* to the ending balance on the log. If they are not, you *should determine* where the problem is and correct it before proceeding.	On the appropriate line of the Audit Control log, *write* the totals printed in the register for Accounts Receivable and Collections. The beginning balance on the register *should equal* the ending balance on the log. If they are unequal, *determine* where the problem is and correct it before proceeding.

Fig. 3-10 Misusing *should* may cause confusion. Use *should* only for stating desired results of conditions.

Route the wires according to the instructions on the wiring board. Each wire should be laid out straight and parallel in a neat package.

Another example of the conspicuous overuse of conditional statements in manuals is illustrated below. Suppose we have a dial:

Often, its use is explained this way:

If the dial is set on 1, A is obtained.
If the dial is set on 2, B is obtained.
If the dial is set on 3, C is obtained.

Why make the statements conditional? We wonder what the cumulative effect of such a mode of expression, quite common in TME, is on readability and understanding. We suggest that a better way to explain the use of the dial is as follows:

Set dial on 1 for A.
Set dial on 2 for B.
Set dial on 3 for C.

YOU *MUST?*	
Wrong	**Right**
To multiply fractions	*To multiply fractions*
1. You must reduce each fraction to its lowest terms.	1. Reduce each fraction to its lowest terms.
2. You must multiply the numerators to form the numerator of the product.	2. Multiply the numerators to form the numerator of the product.
3. You must multiply the denominators to form the denominator of the product.	3. Multiply the denominators to form the denominator of the product.
4. You must reduce the resulting fraction to lowest terms.	4. Reduce the resulting fraction to lowest terms.

Fig. 3-11   Save the word *must* for emphatic cautions and conditions. Don't use *must* for ordinary procedural steps.

Or,

| Set dial on 1 for A, on 2 for B, on 3 for C.

In addition to beginning every instruction with a specific imperative verb and using conditional statements only for stating desired results, save the word *must* for emphatic cautions and warnings. Why tell the reader continually, as in the left-hand column of Figure 3-11, that he or she "must" do something? Don't use *must* for ordinary procedural steps. Here is an example of the word used acceptably: "The hole must be larger than 2 inches in diameter to pass the cable."

Making Notations about Supporting Graphics. It is important when giving instructions to make sure that the reader is able to visualize hardware and equipment, especially the location of every control or button or switch to be set and the position and location of any parts to be adjusted. In other words show enough of the machine or equipment to enable the reader to know with certainty what to do.

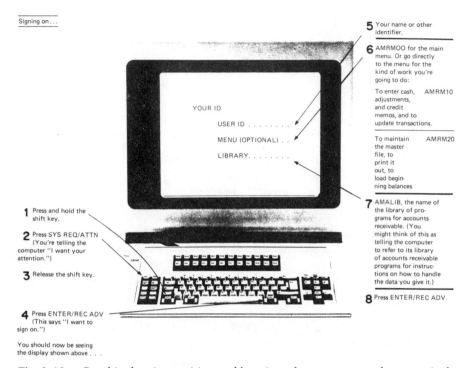

Signing on...

5 Your name or other identifier.

6 AMRMOO for the main menu. Or go directly to the menu for the kind of work you're going to do:

To enter cash,   AMRM10
adjustments,
and credit
memos, and to
update transactions.

To maintain   AMRM20
the master
file, to
print it
out, to
load begin-
ning balances

YOUR ID

USER ID . . . .

MENU (OPTIONAL) . .

LIBRARY. . . . .

7 AMALIB, the name of the library of pro- grams for accounts receivable. (You might think of this as telling the computer to refer to its library of accounts receivable programs for instruc- tions on how to handle the data you give it.)

1 Press and hold the shift key.

2 Press SYS REQ/ATTN (You're telling the computer "I want your attention.")

3 Release the shift key.

8 Press ENTER/REC ADV.

4 Press ENTER/REC ADV (This says "I want to sign on.")

You should now be seeing the display shown above . . .

Fig. 3-12. Graphic showing position and location of parts necessary for a terminal operator to sign on to a computer. (*Courtesy of International Business Machines Corporation*)

In Figure 3-12, for example, is the graphic resulting from a nota-tion like "Show how to sign on [to a computer]." Notice that the instructions point directly to the keys as they appear on the key-board. This method of showing the part where it is located contrasts with the method of showing disembodied keys floating in the text, like this:

  1. Press and hold the shift key ⬆.

Notice that the word *shift* does not even appear on the key. Thus the reader could mistakenly hit another key that has a similar marking—a cursor key, for example.

But you can have too much detail. You must strike a balance between showing enough and showing too much. Exclude details

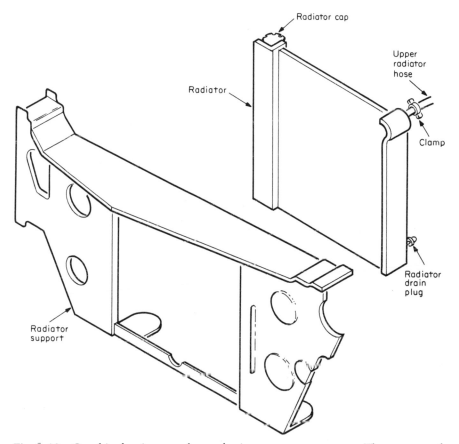

Fig. 3-13   Graphic that incorrectly emphasizes an extraneous part. The purpose of the graphic is to show the location of the upper radiator hose.

that are irrelevant. For instance, when referring to some part of an automobile radiator, emphasize that part and that area. Do not obscure what you are pointing out by including extraneous details. For example, in the graphic in Figure 3-13, it is not necessary to show the radiator support detailed as completely as the radiator itself. The purpose of the illustration is to show where the clamp for the upper radiator hose is.

It is even more important to illustrate difficult points when your instructions concern software, or computer programs, and other subjects that are not visible as are machines and hardware. You will be doing the reader a service if you can make these subjects visible and

DATA IN BATCHES

A batch is a number of things grouped for some purpose. The idea of a batch is nothing new to you. You also know that there can be a limit to the number of things batched. A record player, for example, may allow you to stack (batch) only ten records at a time.

The computer too has a batch limit. It can take in only so many items (usually records) at one time (in one batch). It then asks you to put the remainder in other batches.

Handling records in batches has several advantages. Knowing what batch a record is in lets you find it faster. And, for keeping track of things, it's easier to do it by batches. They're more manageable.

The computer lets you know when you are approaching its batch limit (or capacity) by sending you a message like this:

WARNING: BATCH FILE APPROACHING CAPACITY

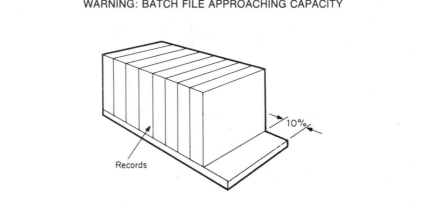

Fig. 3-14 Graphics can be used to help the reader visualize software or other abstract entities that are not visible as are machines and hardware.

understandable. How? We can relate such subjects to familiar objects or more concrete objects. The graphic in Figure 3-14, for example, is how the writer might handle the first appearance of the word *batch* as used in data processing. The notation on the task detail sheet might be phrased something like "Show and relate the word *batch* to a group of items on a shelf."

Because we have stressed graphics so strongly here, a word of caution is necessary. It is to a large extent true that "a picture is worth a thousand words." Certainly we are moved by photographs

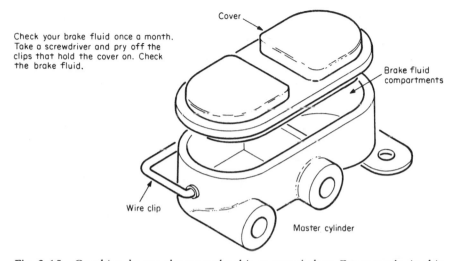

Check your brake fluid once a month. Take a screwdriver and pry off the clips that hold the cover on. Check the brake fluid.

Cover

Brake fluid compartments

Wire clip

Master cylinder

Fig. 3-15 Graphics do not always make things crystal-clear. For example, in this graphic the reader cannot tell how much brake fluid should be in the master cylinder. The accompanying explanation must be more specific (see text).

of, for example, people suffering from war and disaster. Such pictures are often more eloquent than words. But when it comes to making technical matters clear, we must not fall into the trap of thinking that pictures always make everything crystal-clear, and that we can skimp on the explanation in words.

For example, in Figure 3-15 is a graphic intended to show the reader how to service a car's master cylinder. "Check your brake fluid once a month." Fine. But *what* are we supposed to look for, and what are we supposed to do about it? Let us add the few words that will enable the reader to do the job properly:

Check your brake fluid once a month. Take a screwdriver and pry off the clips that hold the cover on. Pour in enough fluid to keep both compartments filled to within ¼ inch of the top.

Few pictures are self-explanatory. Don't forget that a picture is an *equal* partner of words, not a replacement for them.

Now that we have expressed a word of caution about skimping on words when using graphics, let us discuss myths and fallacies that inhibit the use of graphics. These beliefs perpetuate themselves through inertia and tradition: "You can't do that because it's never been done before." How many times have you heard that?

An example is the myth that says you can't cross the middle of a binder (where the rings are) with a graphic presentation or layout. As a matter of fact, there are times when you will want to take advantage of the sweeping panorama offered by a standard opened binder, which spans 17 inches from left to right. Such a layout is illustrated in Figure 3-16.

If you are to create effective technical manuals in an age of great illiteracy and of increasing reluctance to read *anything,* let alone a technical manual, then you must challenge the validity of these stifling notions. As another example, we hear "You should not use graphics for the sake of using graphics." In fact, there are times when that is exactly what you should do. In this age of television, this epoch of the visual image, to reach your restless audiences you must avoid the ponderous, soporific look of dozens of pages of solid text.

Next to a page of solid text, contrast the impression conveyed by Figure 3-17. Here we see a page in which a "theme" picture has been added. A theme picture is one that is connected by theme, by general feeling or mood, rather than directly, with the subject at hand. Note that the graphic is not given a figure number, nor is it captioned. It is a graphic for the sake of using a graphic. The reasoning is as follows: When a reader is crossing a dry desert of prose, he or she needs a visual oasis at which to stop and take a visual drink . . . before continuing across the desert of prose. In other words, it is a deliberate attempt to break up the prose and change the pace.

Take advantage of the many opportunities you have, through graphics, to make your writing clearer, more effective, more pleasant, easier to digest. As you fill out the task detail sheet, ask yourself these questions:

- Are the words of this instruction clear?
- Could the person in the next office carry out the instruction without difficulty?
- Would an illustration help make the instruction clearer?

In this book, you will find numerous illustrations that may help you think of better ways to say it graphically. You have only to find them and apply them.

Amplifying the Instructions. You can use the fourth column of the task detail sheet to state warnings and cautions or to jot down any ideas that might help you amplify the instruction stated in the second column. These entries might include statements concerning any difficulty you observe when the reader performs the step. Such a note would serve as a signal for you to write detailed directions explaining how to carry out an instruction stated in the second column. Or the fourth column might include explanations of what the reader is to do if something fails at that particular point in the procedure—a contingency.

Such additional information becomes very important at times, and you'll have to develop a sense of when to amplify your instructions to help the reader work accurately, safely, and confidently. A little reflection will remind you of the reader's plight. Take, for instance, the budding shade-tree mechanic who is learning how to clean battery cable connectors and battery posts. Removing the cables from the posts is simple for one who already knows how to do it. Thus, the instruction "Disconnect the cables from the battery posts" appears clear enough—if you already know the procedure. The question is, will the reader know it? A lot of beginners, suspecting that electricity flows from the battery to other parts of the ignition system, may be reluctant to touch the battery with a wrench or screwdriver. So you need to show them how to remove the cables and explain to them that although they might draw a spark from the battery there's no shock. In certain situations, though, the reader might not even want the spark; so show how to unhook the cable from the negative post first (if the battery is negative ground). Keep asking yourself: I've told the reader *what* to do. Have I shown the reader *how* to do it?[1]

There will be times when the reader is likely to experience difficulty in performing the procedure. The best approach, of course, is to warn of conditions that are potentially troublesome, injurious, or damaging. If you anticipate the reader's problems, explain how to get

---

[1]If you need additional help on how to recognize the assumptions you make in writing instructions, see a landmark article by Joseph Racker titled "Selecting and Writing to the Proper Level," (*IEEE Transactions on Engineering Writing and Speech*, EWS-2, no. 1, January 1959, pp. 16–21), which discusses how even the simplest instruction assumes considerable knowledge on the part of the reader.

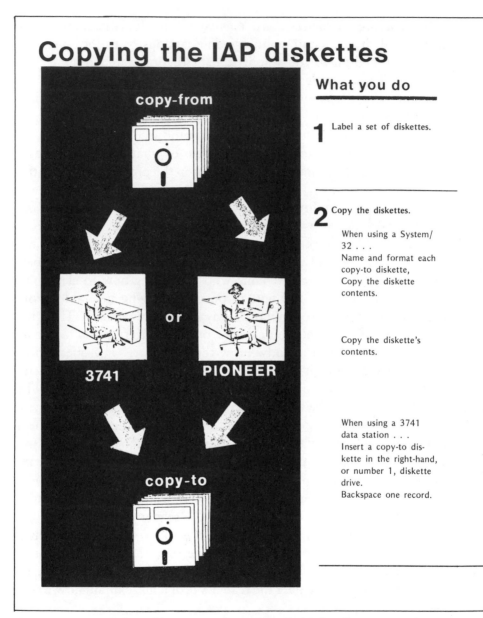

Copying the IAP diskettes

copy-from

3741 **or** **PIONEER**

copy-to

What you do

1 Label a set of diskettes.

2 Copy the diskettes.

When using a System/ 32 . . .
Name and format each copy-to diskette,
Copy the diskette contents.

Copy the diskette's contents.

When using a 3741 data station . . .
Insert a copy-to diskette in the right-hand, or number 1, diskette drive.
Backspace one record.

Fig. 3-16 Layout achieved by crossing the middle of a binder allows you to double the size of the page. (*Courtesy of International Business Machines Corporation*)

The why and how

For example...

Repeat the label and add PIONEER in bold letters so that the copy-to diskettes cannot be confused with the original (copy-from) diskettes.

Name the diskette and format it (if necessary) using the INIT command. Take the name, volume-ID, and owner-ID, from the diskette display of the copy-from diskette. Use the FORMAT parameter for formatting. To display a diskette, enter the CATALOG command.

Use the COPYI1 command. ALL is the default, so you need enter only the vol-id paramater. Double-check to see that the respective diskettes are used for each copy.

Backspacing one record to the 0007 header record automatically copies the copy-from diskette name, volume ID, and owner ID, to the copy-to diskette. Be sure that the copy-to diskettes are in the standard interchange format (see the INIT command).

This diskette is controlled by the upper-function select, or green, key and legend. Press the upper function select key each time you press the record advance key. If you advance a record too far and get a blinking display, just reset and backspace one record.

3740 Data Entry System (magnetic IBM Diskettes)

Step 1. Make your key decisions early

Where are you now?

If you are already running another System/32 manufacturing application, you will find some of this book repetitive. However, because there are important differences between the various applications, you should read the entire book.

Where to put your System/32

There will be no surprises and no last-minute movement of people if you decide now exactly where your new computer will be placed.

- It is only slightly larger than a standard office desk.
- It needs no more air conditioning than you and your people do to work comfortably.
- Its only special requirement is for a particular kind of electrical outlet similar to the kind you have installed for your clothes dryer at home.

But you will want to have adequate workspace for your operator and a place where the reference books supplied by IBM can be kept near at hand.

Refer to the physical planning manual, GA21-9177, for specific information, and consult your IBM representative.

Job responsibilities

The operator's job

To ensure a smooth, fast, and efficient installation of your system, it is important that the right people be assigned to the right tasks, now. Your operator must be able to run the Sales Analysis application on your

System/32 and perform the following types of tasks:
- Determine the procedure to be run
- Assemble input data and forms
- Initiate the correct procedures
- Initiate responses to system prompts
- Enter data into the system through the keyboard
- Verify control totals at the end of the job
- Distribute job results

You should also consider training a backup operator as insurance against the loss of your regular operator.

The supervisor's job

A supervisor must be able to manage the installation and operation of Sales Analysis. You should be familiar with your company's policies, business practices, and Sales Analysis operation. Although you need not be experienced in the use and installation of data processing systems, you should be able to successfully carry out any of the following tasks:
- Provide answers to the Questionnaire (Step 4)
- Select and supervise one or more operators
- Be the responsible authority for sales analysis in your company

Fig. 3-17   Use a theme picture to break up the solid text. (*Reprinted by permission from International Business Machines Corporation*)

out of them. To do this, the if-then formula works well. Here are two examples.

If the waveforms are not in the same time sequence, reverse the T_4 primary leads.

Plug the soldering iron in the ac outlet. *Caution:* If this is the first time the tip has been used, put a coating of solder on the tip as soon as the tip is hot enough to melt solder. To coat the tip, simply touch it with solder until the solder melts. Coating with solder allows the tip to conduct heat to the joint efficiently and prolongs the life of the tip.

That last sentence is a good example of explaining why something must be done. Readers sometimes have the attitude of "it doesn't seem reasonable that I should do it this way." Explaining *why* prevents a lot of mistakes.

Another situation in which you might need to amplify an instruction is when there are alternatives to be weighed by the reader. Plan Sheet I: The Alternatives Sheet (see Figures 3-18 and 3-19), shows an expansion of the material for step 1 of the task detail sheet (Figure 3-6). See also Chapters 4 and 5 for additional information on showing alternatives in complicated procedures.

Here again, as with the other plan sheets, you should impose a rigid discipline: Do not state alternatives unless their relative advantages and disadvantages are thoroughly discussed so that the reader can make an intelligent decision. You may want to design other plan sheets in addition to the alternatives sheet to support instructions. Each additional plan sheet would fill a specific communicative role in supporting a specific instruction, as the alternatives sheet serves to explain alternatives.

If you keep an eye open for obstacles the reader may have to overcome or for places where the reader may have to make a decision, you will be able to explain exactly how to perform the work, how to take preventive or corrective action, and how and why to make a decision.

Validating the Filled-Out Plan Sheets H and I

Once the task detail sheet (Plan Sheet H) and the alternatives sheet (Plan Sheet I) are filled out, you have broken down the job into bite-sized components. You will know what you need to write about in the procedural part of the manual, and you will have the information you need to write it. Now you test whether you have met the objective with the information given on the task detail sheet.

You have already verified the information with the subject-matter experts. Now you need to validate the information by testing whether your intended reader can *use* it. The question of who will

PLAN SHEET I:
THE ALTERNATIVES SHEET

Procedure _____

Method	Advantages	Disadvantages
1.		
2.		
3.		

Fig. 3-18   Plan Sheet I: The Alternatives Sheet.

	PLAN SHEET I:	
	THE ALTERNATIVES SHEET	

Choose which method you want for doing your receivables.

Method	Advantages	Disadvantages
1. Balance forward. You keep a running record of all transactions for 1 month. Statements show every transaction that occurred in the *current* month, but only a balance brought forward from previous statements.	Faster and more flexible in the number of different data arrangements made possible. Results in prompter collections of receivables through. . . .	Requires an extra 47 characters per account. Most customers prefer to receive the more complete details not provided through this method. In a recent survey. . . .
2. Open item. Keeps a running record of *all* transactions—invoices, adjustments, cash receipts, etc.)—until they are accounted for. Statements show every transaction that remains outstanding—however long that might be.	Most customers prefer the kind of statements available from the open-item method. In addition, it. . . .	Requires an extra person to tabulate the transactions according to current data and. . . .
3. Both balance forward *and* open item. Balance forward for most customers and open item for a few, or vice versa.	Allows you to select which customers are more suited for one kind of handling than another. Also, it uses less. . . .	Requires the running of an extra procedure, which takes about 30 minutes for 6000 accounts.

Fig. 3-19   Example of a filled-out Plan Sheet I.

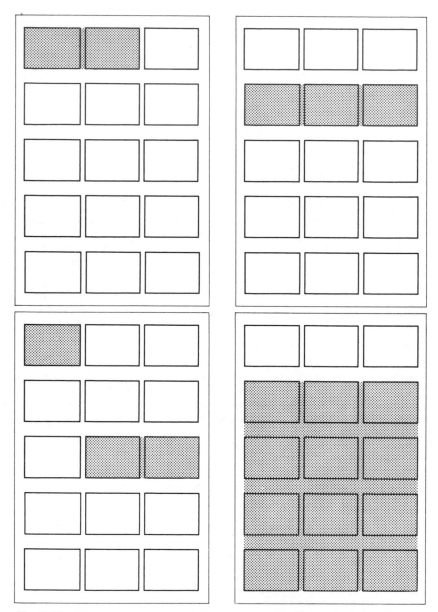

Fig. 3-20 You can construct a grid to any page size. Pictured are four layouts on a typical grid for a 8½ by 11 inch page. Fifteen modules are used, arbitrarily. The shaded areas indicate a photograph or other graphics.

test instructions is very important. Try to find an uninformed person (typical of your intended audience) to test as the user of the instructions. There is no reason why you should get the best-qualified person to check your writing. After all, you already have the subject-matter experts involved in this, and they aren't the audience anyway. Your audience is likely to have priorities, pressures, goals, and backgrounds that are considerably different from your own or those of the subject-matter experts.

When Tolstoy finished a passage of *War and Peace*, it is reported that he would go down into the kitchen, read the passage to a servant, and ask the servant if he or she could understand it. It was not beneath Tolstoy's dignity to attempt to make his writing clear to anyone. That's your goal too: making your instructions so clear that anyone can understand them. So check whether you have met your objective, arrange a simulation using somebody who might qualify as a *beginning user*. If that person can perform the task, you have met the objective. If you haven't met your objective, rewrite and retest the instructions until you *do* meet it.

Completed and tested, the task detail sheet and the alternatives sheet present the step-by-step procedure in a format and style very close to what will appear in the published manual. All you need to do is have your graphics experts refine the use of space and the illustrations. We suggest that you work with your graphics department to build your manual page layout on a grid (see Figure 3-20). A grid is simply a basic pattern underlying the layout of a page. The layouts of the task detail and the alternatives sheets are examples of grids. As they are, they may be suitable for your purposes. What is the advantage of a grid? Simply this: It makes laying out of material easier, because it gives you an underlying structure to build on. Your pages may take many different layouts, as shown in Figure 3-20, but despite the variety of layouts there is an underlying unity and harmony imposed by the unchanging basic grid.

For more information about increasing the visual impact of the manual, see Chapter 5.

FOUR

Explaining How to Fix the Product

The product your manual supports is designed and manufactured to be as reliable as good business practice permits. Nevertheless breakdowns do occur, because no product or user is perfect. When something goes wrong—because of unforeseen circumstances or human error—your reader will turn to your manual for a clear path through the maze of possible faults, symptoms, and remedies. To keep repair time and costs low, your manual must contain maintenance information to help the reader (either the operator or the service person) fix the product quickly and correctly, as somebody will be keeping a close watch until it is fixed.

How much information to include in the maintenance section of the manual can be a problem. It is, of course, impossible to include every potential problem. Even if you could conceive of every potential problem, you wouldn't want to include all of them because your reader would probably become overly concerned about the liability of the product or become exasperated over the complexity of identifying various problems, diagnosing multiple faults, and knowing what materials and tools to use in making repairs. On the other hand, if you omit *important* faults, your reader may not find help when it is needed most.

In selecting maintenance information, work closely with subject-matter experts who have designed and tested the product. They will have amassed a lot of information from testing the product. Also, stay in touch with customers who keep performance records on the product and with field-service personnel familiar with the product. They will have invaluable field experience with the product.

After you and the subject-matter experts have compiled a list of symptoms, faults, and remedies, design a format for presenting the maintenance information. There's no fail-safe guide that tells you what format is best, but consider the following points:

• Get the information across in as few words as possible. When your reader must diagnose a problem, he or she doesn't want a dissertation on the theory of operation.

• Use some form of the two most common formats for maintenance information—the troubleshooting table and the decision tree. Traditional prose can be too complex for the reader who is concentrating on a clear path to the identity and solution of a problem. Tables and decision trees are more explicit, use a minimum of words, and take less space.

• Use symbols that are easy to read. The type of symbols you use will be determined by your audience—the lay reader (operator or do-it-yourselfer) or the technician (who earns a living making repairs). Use as few different symbols as possible (sometimes rectangles and arrows are enough), because the more symbols you use the more symbol meanings your reader will have to learn.

The key to presenting maintenance information is to use a format that helps the reader untangle relevant from irrelevant information. As the reader identifies the factors relevant to a particular situation, he or she can ignore the irrelevant factors and thus reduce the load on memory. You must decide whether a troubleshooting chart or a decision tree best serves your reader, on the basis of the kind of format the reader is familiar with.

THE TROUBLESHOOTING TABLE

Plan Sheet J: The Troubleshooting Table (Figure 4-1) has four main columns. Traditionally, the column heads of a troubleshooting table

PLAN SHEET J:
THE TROUBLESHOOTING TABLE

You notice	This may mean	Caused by	You should

Fig. 4-1 Plan Sheet J: The Troubleshooting Table.

might read something like "Trouble," "Symptom," "Cause"; or "Problem," "Source of Problem," "Possible Cause"; or "Remedy," "Solution," "Action." We recommend our suggested heads, because they keep the reader in the picture.

Do not crowd the layout. In the heat of action, the reader will move back and forth between the work and the troubleshooting table. Therefore, the text must be surrounded by plenty of white space for easy reading. Plenty of white space between the columns and between the rows also leaves room for the reader to make notations. Figure 4-2 illustrates typical entries.

The First Column ("You Notice")

When possible, use phrases and sentence fragments rather than whole sentences in the first column. Put a period or don't put a period after each entry, but whichever way you go, be consistent (see Figure 4-3).

Arrange the symptoms by order of frequency of occurrence.

To describe the trouble well, specify the possible symptom as accurately as possible. Try to describe exactly what the reader is likely to see, hear, or smell. For example, the single word "Hum" may be replaced with the more descriptive "Hum when volume is turned down" or "Hum when volume is turned up"—whichever is the case. Dividing the symptom enables the reader to isolate the cause of the trouble faster. Another troublesome description of a symptom associated with electronic equipment is "a popping noise." The words "for several seconds" would clarify the symptom, and not make it appear as though something were wrong when the receiver popped only once when it was turned on. A single pop may be a natural occurrence in such equipment.

The Second Column ("This May Mean")

In the second column, use phrases such as the one shown in Figure 4-4. Arrange the items in the order of frequency, and number them. Punctuate consistently; either use periods after all items, or use no periods.

PLAN SHEET J:
THE TROUBLESHOOTING TABLE

You notice	This may mean	Caused by	You should
A click-click-click—but nothing happens	You have enough electricity to activate the starter solenoid; but not enough to turn the starter over	Corroded battery terminals A weak battery A defective starter	Clean terminals and re-tighten cables Use jumper cable to start car Recharge battery Have a qualified mechanic check out the problem

Fig. 4-2 Typical entries for a troubleshooting table.

You notice	This may mean	Caused by	You should
Oil filter drain plug breaks when you attempt to remove it.	....	....	....

Fig. 4-3 A typical entry for the first column of the troubleshooting table.

The Third Column ("Caused By")

In the third column, use phrases such as those shown in Figure 4-5. Arrange the items in the order of frequency, as shown in Figure 4-6. When possible, in referring to a component (as in item 3 listed in Figure 4-6) identify it with a number keyed to a schematic diagram, a parts list, or some other illustration. Don't forget, however, that schematic and other *technical* diagrams are intended for technical audiences only. Be sure to explain the number in parentheses to your reader.

The Fourth Column ("You Should")

In the fourth column, arrange the remedies according to the frequency with which the problem occurs (see Figure 4-7). All the principles of good instructions, which we discussed in Chapter 3, apply here.

- Start the sentence with an imperative verb.
- Make your instruction complete. Don't say, "Replace if worn." Rather, say something like "Replace if worn more than ¼ inch."

You notice	This may mean	Caused by	You should
....	**1.** Plug seizes in the drain hole.	....	....

Fig. 4-4 A typical entry for the second column of the troubleshooting table.

You notice	This may mean	Caused by	You should
. . . .	. . . .	Wrong kind of plug used. Perhaps an aluminum plug is used. The chemical reaction between the two different metals causes the plug to seize in the hole.	. . . .

Fig. 4-5 A typical entry for the third column of the troubleshooting table.

Caused by
1. Defect in filter circuit.
2. Float on float switch is jammed upward.
3. Microswitch activating arm is broken or bent (S508M).

Fig. 4-6 In the third column of the troubleshooting table, arrange possible causes in the order of frequency. Identify components by a number keyed to a schematic, a parts list, or some other illustration.

You notice	This may mean	Caused by	You should
. . . .	. . . .	. . . .	1. Test cycle switch S1531 (use voltmeter 31-A). 2. Tighten oscillator belt (use special tool Z-47).

Fig. 4-7 A typical entry for the fourth column of the troubleshooting table.

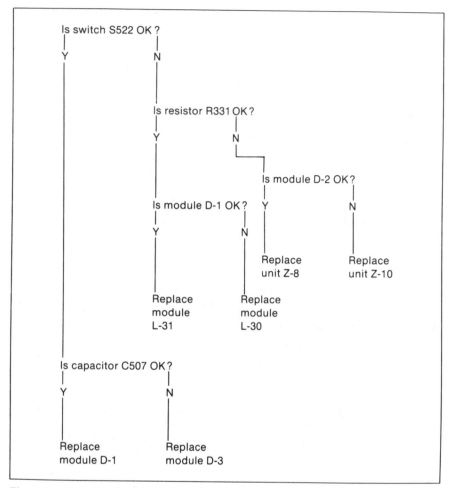

Fig. 4-8 A decision tree.

- Remember to fit the instruction to the knowledge of the reader. For an operator, the remedy should not exceed his or her occupational knowledge. That is, the machine operator should not be asked to use an oscilloscope or other complex apparatus to diagnose and fix a problem. When such a situation exists, let the remedy state "Call your service representative" or some other appropriate person. If the instruction is for the technician, specify what kind of test equipment or special tools will be needed (see Figure 4-7). Include an illustration, such as an exploded view, to help the reader find parts.

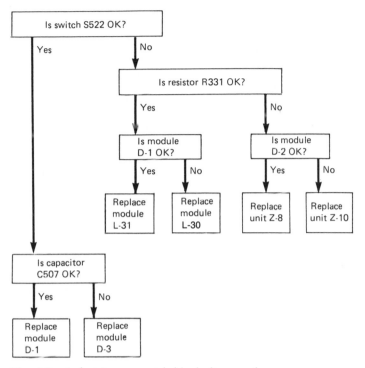

Fig. 4-9   A decision tree with block diagram features.

In writing the instruction, determine whether a statement like "Test cycle switch S1531 (use voltmeter 31-A)" is all your reader needs to do the job. If so, you do not have to go into the details of performing the test. However, if the reader needs the detailed instruction for testing cycle switch S1531, the best method is to present it as part of the prescribed remedy. Try to avoid having the reader direct his or her attention to another section of the manual for the test instruction. However, if you cannot include the detailed instruction with the remedy, place it on a facing page or clearly indicate where the instruction may be found.

THE DECISION TREE

Although the troubleshooting table is a good form for listing symptoms, faults, and remedies, you might consider it as the basis for developing another type of graphic that aids in diagnosing faults: the decision tree (sometimes called the yes-no chart). This widely used chart, shown in Figure 4-8, is excellent for identifying faults and helping the reader decide what steps should be taken to correct them.

Another action chart derived from the decision tree is shown in Figure 4-9, in which we've incorporated the block diagram and arrow line features of the more familiar flowchart.

For locating faulty areas and identifying solutions, tables and charts are easier to follow than straight text. Use them.

FIVE

Mapping the Manual

Working at improving your writing can lead to a curious paradox. The very activity that improves writing—attention to words— brings its own special problem: inattention to graphic impact. And although throughout this book we have integrated discussion of graphics into places where we felt it would be most useful, we want to devote this chapter to showing how graphics can make the difference between a well-designed and a poorly designed manual.

By *mapping* we mean organizing the information and laying it out so as to make it easier to find, read, and understand. We want to avoid, if at all possible, the formidable look of solid text. Say it with graphics.

By *graphics* we mean not only pictures but also the typographical layout of the page and its information. As an example from a recent article shows, even without the use of pictures solid text can sometimes be translated into a more graphic presentation (see Figure 5-1). Even with such a simple "graphic" transformation, the gain in communicative effectiveness is great.

HOW TO MAP

Mapping should become a natural part of your writing, and you should develop your own way of mapping. We offer the following procedure as a starter.

Difficult to read	Easier to read
When time is limited, travel by Rocket, unless cost is also limited, in which case go by Space Ship. When only cost is limited, an Astrobus should be used for journeys of less than 10 orbs, and a Satellite for longer journeys. Cosmocars are recommended when there are no constraints on time or cost, unless the distance to be traveled exceeds 10 orbs. For journeys longer than 10 orbs, when time and cost are not important, journeys should be made by Super Star.	When only time is limited travel by Rocket. When only cost is limited travel by Satellite if journey is more than 10 orbs; travel by Astrobus if journey is less than 10 orbs. When both time and cost are limited travel by Space Ship. When time and cost are not limited travel by Super Star if journey is more than 10 orbs; travel by Cosmocar if journey is less than 10 orbs.

Fig. 5-1 Human factors research conducted by Patricia Wright indicates that a list of short sentences is easier to understand than a traditional prose passage. (See Patricia Wright, "Behavioral Research and Technical Communication," *The Communicator of Scientific and Technical Information*, no. 32, July 1977, p. 5. See also Patricia Wright, "Behavioral Research and the Technical Communicator," *Technical Communication*, no. 25, second quarter, 1978, pp. 6–12.)

First, analyze the prose to determine whether it can be divided into categories by some criteria. Two parts, of course, is the simplest and sometimes the most effective division. This elementary analysis will enable you to form at least a basic map, such as the one illustrated in Figure 5-2. Here are some suggested two-part classifications:

Important vs. unimportant
Action vs. result (reaction)
Instructional vs. factual
Definitional vs. functional
Sequenced vs. random
Simple vs. complex
Part vs. whole
General vs. specific

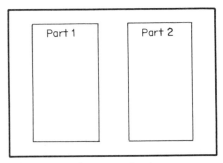

Fig. 5-2 Use a simple two-part classification to develop a basic map.

Frequent vs. infrequent
Presence vs. absence
Changeable vs. permanent
Interior vs. exterior
Insertion vs. extraction
Visibility vs. invisibility
Inquiry vs. answer
Assent vs. dissent
Good vs. bad
Before vs. after
Success vs. failure
Support vs. opposition
Acquisition vs. loss
Giving vs. receiving
Advantages vs. disadvantages
Required vs. optional
Random vs. ordered
One time only vs. ongoing
Material vs. immaterial
Prompt vs. response
Familiar vs. unfamiliar
Skilled vs. unskilled

Second, analyze the prose for graphic possibilities. An action performed by a person, for example, may suggest an action picture such as that shown in Figure 5-3.

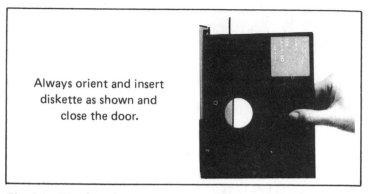

Always orient and insert
diskette as shown and
close the door.

Fig. 5-3   Words and graphics should be equal partners in conveying information. For instance, an action performed by a person may best be presented verbally and graphically. (*Courtesy of International Business Machines Corporation*)

Third, using as an underlying guide the concept of grids described in Chapter 3, try several combinations of text and graphics, such as those illustrated in Figure 5-4.

Now let's look at how to convert a textual presentation into a more graphic presentation.

At first glance, the copy in Figure 5-5 seems to defy an analysis for mapping. A closer look, however, reveals certain possibilities.

First, we realize that this succinct passage is a check-off list, not a set of instructions, even though the sentences are written as commands. The entries tell the reader what to do, but do not show the reader *how* to do it. Much more information should be provided for each step.

Second, there is a prompt-response relationship in what is being conveyed in the writing, although in this version that all-important distinction is blurred. That is, the machine prompts the operator, who then responds in some manner. This suggests at least a two-part division of information: prompt and response.

Third, remembering the suggestion about translating information to make it meaningful to the reader, we realize that the prompts may not always give a clear idea of what the reader is to do in response. Translating the machine's prompts to the operator is crucial in this instance. This suggests that perhaps a three-part division of the infor-

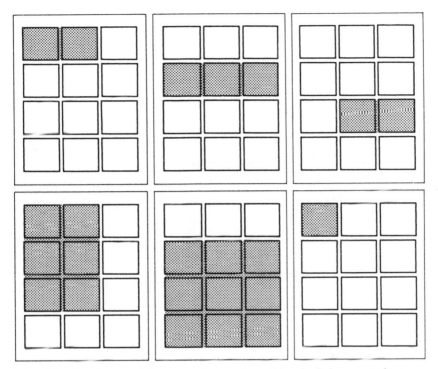

Fig. 5-4 Develop a grid to map instructions. The shaded areas indicate a photograph or other graphics.

mation would be effective: prompt, explanation of the prompt, and the response.

Fourth, there is much evidence to suggest that copy should not be in all capital letters. It creates a ponderous appearance.

After some further thought and discussion, we decide to create a basic map consisting of three columns, as shown in Figure 5-6. Once a map is established, it is repeated for every procedure or operation in the manual. This repetition creates consistency and predictability, which builds the reader's confidence.

HOW TO MAP A COMPLICATED PROCEDURE

What can you do when your task is to explain a procedure that is so complicated that it looks like the one in Figure 5-7? In this instance,

GETTING ON-LINE WITH THE COMPUTER

- ACTIVATE CRT.
- PRESS RUBOUT KEY.
- TYPE IN ACCOUNT NAME.
- PRESS RETURN KEY.
- TYPE IN PASSWORD.
- IF ACCOUNT NUMBER OR PASSWORD IS REJECTED, PRESS RUBOUT AND RETYPE ACCOUNT NAME AND PASSWORD.
- TO ACCESS DESIRED PROGRAM, GO TO ACCESSING AND RUNNING PROGRAM ROUTINE.

and so on.

Fig. 5-5 Instructions like these are undesirable for several reasons. The information has not been mapped to show the prompt-response nature of the instructions. Some of the most important information (what the operator sees on the screen) is missing, because no graphics are included. The text in all capital letters makes the typed information look ponderous.

the reader could take any one of several paths to do the job. Should you explain *every* conceivable path fully? Not if you want to create a usable manual.

The solution is to pick *one* path that works and is simple and easy to follow. Explain that path in a step-by-step fashion, as described in Chapter 4. Do not try to explain every path the reader could take. Not only is it unnecessary, but it would so overcomplicate and overinflate the manual as to render it unusable.

To repeat: Give your reader *one* straightforward way to go and explain it clearly in detail.

How then could you document the remaining paths in an understandable way? We propose an approach that we call the *road map.* Here's why. To understand a complicated procedure, readers must always have the total picture of it in mind. Readers must know not only where they came from and where they are going, but also the *direction* they came from and the direction they are going. If the readers cannot perceive that total picture, at all times, they will fail to understand the explanation because they will lose the way. The road map shows the way.

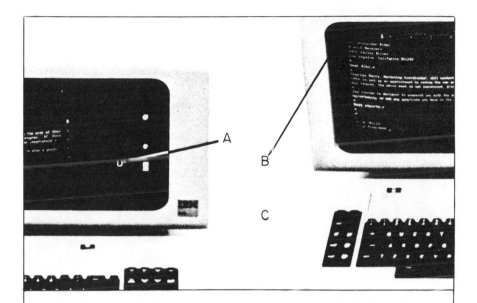

GETTING ON-LINE WITH THE COMPUTER

Step 1

To turn on the display, flip up the red power switch (A above) to ON.

The machine does	This means	You do
Step 2 A small blinking block appears in the top left-hand corner of the screen, as shown in B above.	The computer is ready for you to sign on.	Press and hold the shift key. Press SYS REQ/ATTN. (You're telling the computer "I want your attention.") Release the shift key. Press ENTER/REC ADV. (This says "I want to sign on.")
Step 3 The sign-on display appears.	The computer is waiting for you to identify yourself and pick the job you want to do.	

Fig. 5-6   A map using a three-column format.(*Courtesy of International Business Machines Corporation*)

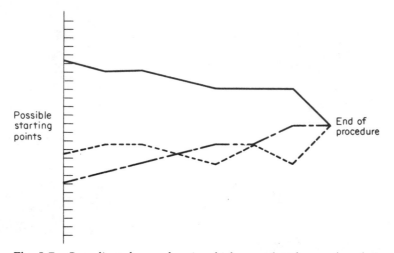

Possible
starting
points

End of
procedure

Fig. 5-7   Complicated procedure in which several paths may be taken
to perform the procedure.

The components of the road map shown in Figures 5-8 to 5-10
illustrate a way to give the reader the total picture of how to begin
and how to proceed to the end of the job. Through this strategy—
having a basic foldout page (or several foldout pages) that match
with a number of pages from the right-hand side—it is possible to
explain complex procedures *one at a time,* with economy and effi-
ciency. If the manual is poorly assembled and the reader cannot find
the way from one point of the procedure to another, it will give the
impression that everything—the product, the procedures, the manual—is, at best, difficult to use, at worst, unreliable.

The left-hand foldout page (Figure 5-8) can be a diagram showing
the origin or starting point of a process or procedure and the major
jobs that can be done, organized by product or by some other classification.

The left-hand matching pages (Figure 5-9) can be a series of pages
with diagrams that match up with the diagram on the folded-out
page. Thus, the reader sees the whole procedure from beginning to
end.

The right-hand facing page or pages (Figure 5-10) can be used to
present detailed instructions or factual data pertinent to the job.

Such a map makes it easy for the reader. Assume that the reader
has opened the manual to the foldout shown in Figure 5-11, and that

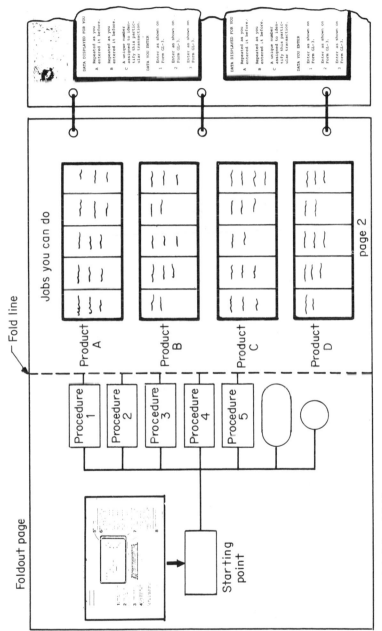

Fig. 5-8 A left-hand foldout page.

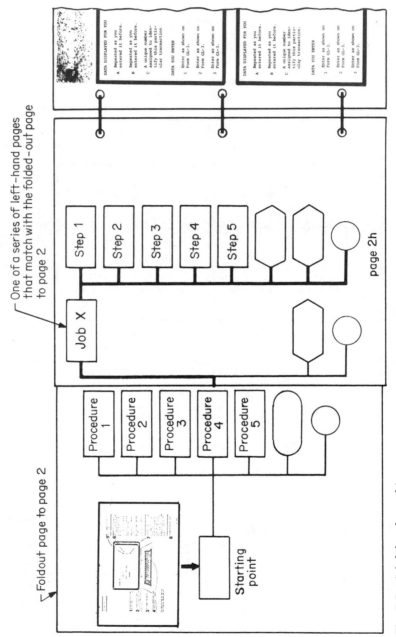

Fig. 5-9 A left-hand matching page.

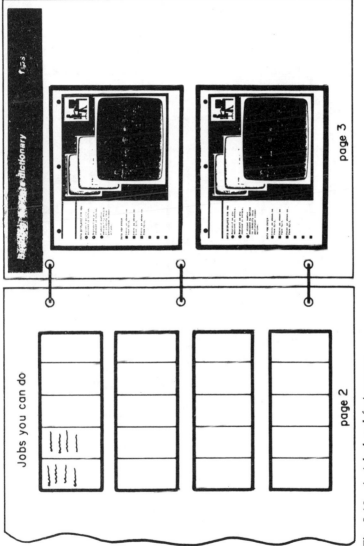

Fig. 5-10 A right-hand facing page.

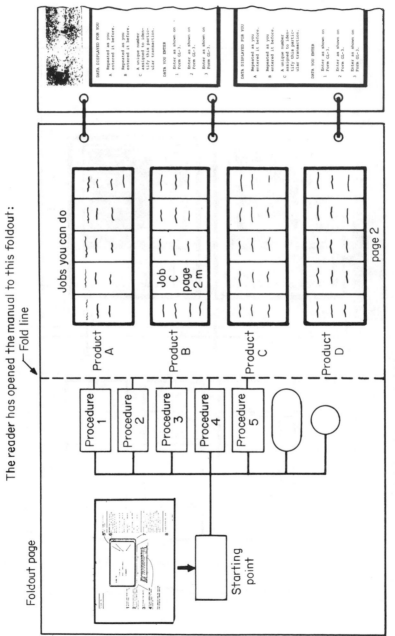

Fig. 5-11 Manual open to left-hand page with foldout.

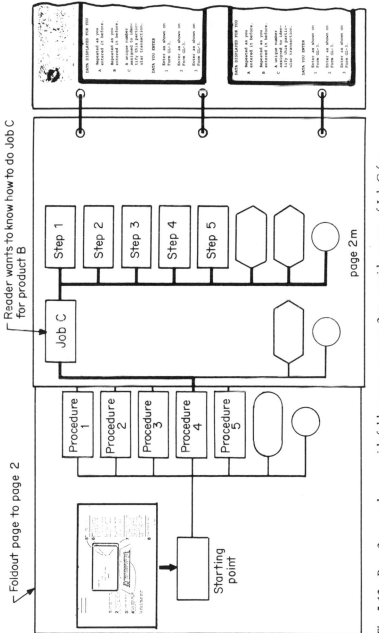

Fig. 5-12 Page 2*m* matches up with foldout page to page 2 to provide a map of Job C for Product B.

he or she is concerned with Product B and, more specifically, how to do Job C for Product B. The diagram refers the reader to page $2m$. When the reader turns page $2l$ over, its other side (page $2m$) has a diagram that mates with the foldout page, as in Figure 5-12. Now before the reader is the total picture of how to do the job—from beginning to end.

SIX

Writing for the World of Computers

Recognizing the computer's impact and potential impact on the world in which we live, *Time* magazine named the computer its "Man of the Year" for 1982. Regardless of what field you're in, it will surely be affected to some degree by computers. They are becoming as common as typewriters. You may, in fact, directly use a computer yourself. Or you may use the results from a computer someone else operates. In either case, for you the computer is a fact of life.

Knowing how to communicate with, by, and for the computer and its users also will be an important part of your future. In what follows we offer some thoughts on how to meet that challenge. All examples in this chapter relate to writing instructions for such computer users as data entry operators, auditors, controllers, and accountants, as well as cost analysts who need instructions in running computer applications in accounting. These are among the most widespread computer users and applications today.

Basically there is nothing different in the way you write manuals for computer users and the way you write other manuals. The information presented in the first five chapters of this book applies also to writing for the world of computers. In fact, several examples in the earlier part of this book illustrate the writing of instructions for computer applications.

Everything—and we do mean everything—should be written in plain English. There will, of course, be some computer terms a beginner is likely to need to know, such as *memory*, RAM, ROM, *field*. Define them. But be a bear about fighting information that is so jargon-ridden that it can be understood only by the subject-matter expert who provided the information. Remember that you are serving the needs of a reader who probably feels like he or she is going into a strange country.

Before we go further in this chapter, let's look at some guidelines that will help you make language in computer manuals clearer and easier to respond to. Even the most technical programmer will admit that it is not good communication to thrust computer jargon—words like *initialization, parameter, interface*—on the masses of data processing beginners who will be using computers for the first time. Actually, there are only a couple of dozen such terms. The solution is to replace them, beloved as they are by old-timers, with words that are more comfortable and familiar (and usually shorter). For example, we could replace the term *parameter* with *selection* (or some such word). Already in many fields there are precedents for using simplified language. A physician can use *clavicle* or *collarbone, cholelithiasis* or *gallstones*.

More importantly, we can work hard at preventing the introduction of new terms that are probably not necessary. If the program is an accounting application, we can decide to use no term not in a widely recognized authoritative reference such as McGraw-Hill's *Intermediate Accounting* (4th edition, 1978), by W. B. Meigs, C. E. Johnson, and A. N. Mosich.

Substituting plainer words for the jargon of data processing and not inventing new terms to replace those that are now in common circulation—those that everyone in the business community already knows and understands easily—will make the language less intimidating not only for data processing novices but also for data processing professionals.

Using plain English is going to help immensely the reader of computer manuals. So will carefully packaging information. In the remainder of this chapter we cover the more traditional medium of printed publications, such as kits and manuals; then we discuss some ideas for using the computer's screen as the principal means of learning how to operate the computer and communicate with it.

KITS

We are so accustomed to thinking of the usual manual as a way of conveying technical information that it may not occur to a lot of writers that another means may be more effective, for example, the kit. A kit is a packaging of different forms of information—diskettes, small booklets, audio cassettes, standard-sized sheets, order forms, video cassettes, schedules, training materials, whatever. The kit enables you to put all these dissimilar items together in one coordinated package.

Generally speaking, there are two kinds of kits: a planning and startup kit and an operator's kit. To illustrate our discussion of these kits, we introduce two fictitious names—ABLE, the name of a computer, and BETA, the name of a program that runs on ABLE.

The Planning and Startup Kit

The planning and startup kit has two audiences: the primary audience is the owner of a business, or its manager, or whoever has been designated to handle the financial accounting for the business; the secondary audience is the operator of the computer.

The purposes of this kit are to help the customer plan for the arrival and installation of the computer and its programs, and to bridge the gap between the purchase of the computer and its delivery.

The *cover* of the kit should have a distinctive logo, or design; it may be repeated on every item inside the kit. On the cover shown in Figure 6-1, the design consists of two diagonal stripes. Its purpose is to give the product a unique identity easily discernible in a mass market.

The *contents* of a typical kit are shown in Figure 6-2. Note especially the instructions "How to use this kit." Among the individual items that may be included in a typical kit, as shown in Figure 6-3, are the following.

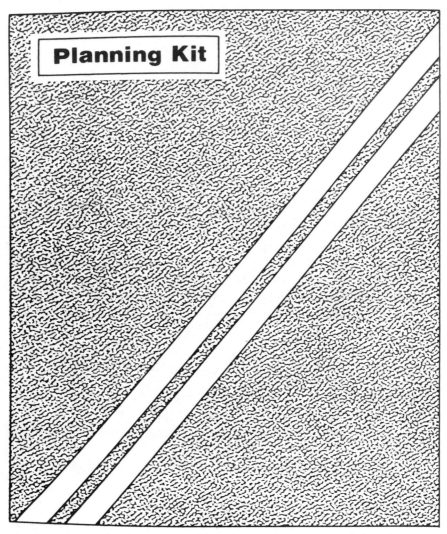

Fig. 6-1   Cover of a planning kit with a distinctive design (two diagonal stripes).

- An installation schedule, which is a fill-in-the-blanks form, or checklist, based on the delivery of the computer and other factors, such as the phasing out of the customer's present system.
- A supplies order form, which is a form the customer fills out and either mails in or gives to the sales representative.
- A training schedule, which contains suggestions and recommenda-

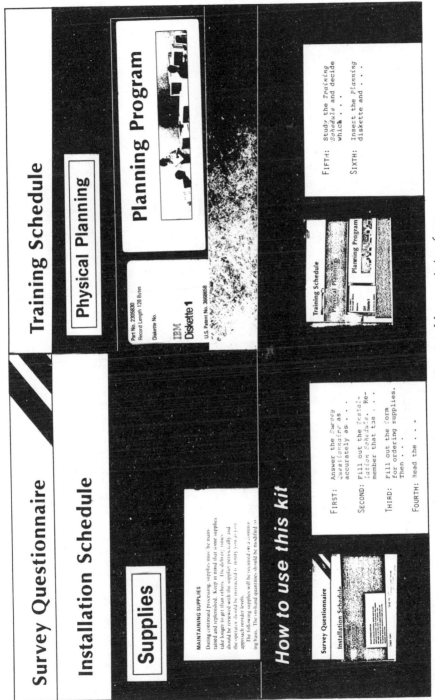

Fig. 6-2 A planning kit opened to show typical contents. *(Reprinted by permission from International Business Machines Corporation)*

Supplies

MAINTAINING SUPPLIES

During continued processing, supplies must be maintained and replenished. Keep in mind that some supplies take longer to get than others. The delivery times should be reviewed with the supplier periodically and the operator should be instructed to notify you as you approach reorder levels.

The following supplies will be required on a continuing basis. The on-hand quantities should be modified to suit your needs:

• Standard computer paper (11" by 14 7/8"). One-part paper to be used in daily processing for reports and listings. Consider using multi-part paper if more than one copy of a report is required.

• Printer ribbons. IBM part number is 1136634, or equivalent. Keep spares on hand.

• Invoice forms. These will take longer to get from your vendor than standard paper. We suggest that you keep at least a 3-month supply on hand, or set up a realistic reorder point with the vendor.

• Order Acknowledgement forms. These also will take longer to get than standard paper. We suggest that you keep at least a 3-month supply on hand or set up a realistic reorder point with the vendor.

• Input forms. These include control logs. The...

ORDER FORM

SEND TO : ALPHA Distribution Center

Telephone

See ordering information at bottom of form

Qty	Order No.	Item	Price *each	10 or more *each	Amount
	2305830	Diskette, singlesided	8.95	7.95	

Installation Schedule

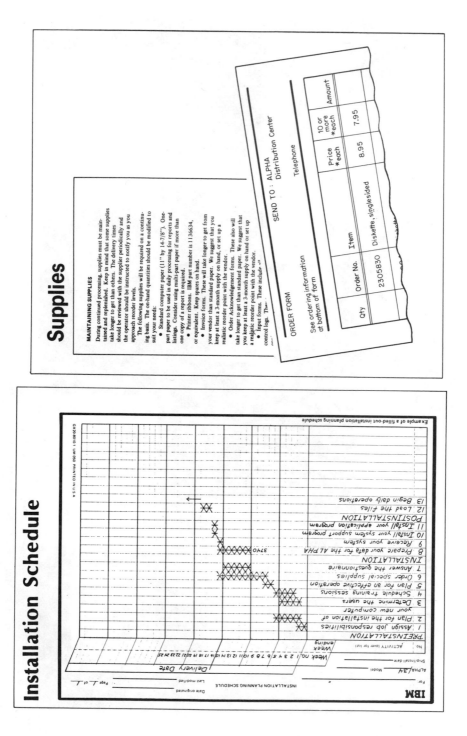

Example of a filled-out installation planning schedule

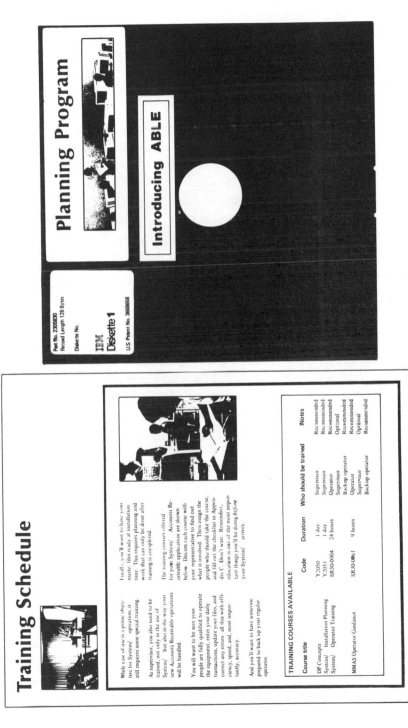

Fig. 6-3 Some of the individual items that may be included in a typical kit. (*Reprinted by permission from International Business Machines Corporation*)

tions on how to prepare and train employees to get the most benefit from the new computer.

- A physical planning guide, which contains recommendations on where to install the computer and its related equipment, supplies, and furniture.

- A booklet, entitled something like *Introducing ABLE,* which is brief—no more than about twenty-five pages—and which explains the product from the customer's point of view: what's in it, how it all relates, how it benefits the business, plus other topics such as, how to hook it up, how to get started, how to load and run a sample program, how to get good results, how to keep a log, how to make a backup copy of your files, how to schedule your work, how to reorder supplies, how to troubleshoot, and other helpful hints.

The Operator's Kit

Like the planning and startup kit, the operator's kit has two audiences. The primary audience is the operator of the computer and anyone designated as a backup operator. The secondary audience is the owner or manager of the business. The contents of this kit should be written so that anyone could take over in an emergency.

The purpose of the operator's kit is to get the operator started and to keep him or her going. The operator must become self-reliant.

As with the other kit, the *cover* (see Figure 6-4) should have a distinctive logo or design. Because of the primary audience, an attractive cover design is also very important here. We suggest keeping in mind the importance of appearing unintimidating, easy to read, and inviting, if possible.

The *contents* of a typical operator's kit are shown in Figure 6-5. Note here too that there are instructions for how to use the kit, displayed prominently at the bottom of the kit. Among the items that may be included in an operator's kit are the following.

- A booklet entitled something like *Introducing BETA*—a short, highly graphic, highly readable booklet on what the program is and does from an operator's point of view. The next main section

Fig. 6-4 Cover of an operator's kit. It too should have a distinctive design that conveys a feeling of friendliness. (*Courtesy of International Business Machines Corporation*)

Fig. 6-5 Contents of a typical operator's kit. Note the placement of instructions for using the kit. (*Courtesy of International Business Machines Corporation*)

of this chapter, in which we explain in detail the writing of such a user's manual, will be of interest in this connection. See Figure 6-6.

- A workbook which contains exercises in running sample problems on the computer. It is designed to take the operator through the various routines of each accounting procedure, or whatever the job may be.

- A quick reference, a small booklet measuring about 4 by 8½ inches, for use at the terminal. Highly graphic, it should contain information and guidance on how to solve common problems in running procedures. It is a troubleshooting tool. Figure 6-7 shows a quick reference manual opened to the data dictionary section. Note the use of page tabs for fast retrieval of information. The quick reference has to be small, because the arm's reach, or conveniently accessible area at the computer terminal, is about 350 square inches. That space is not affected by how big a table the terminal sits on. A standard-sized manual, when open, would occupy over three-fourths of that area, which would leave little room for the operator's source documents, such as invoices and other materials.

The quick reference can be organized in two broad ways: by topics or alphabetically by tasks. Topical organization would contain such entries as backup and recovery, data dictionary, file maintenance, inquiries, menus, procedures, reports, screens, and so forth. Alphabetical organization by task would contain such entries as adjustments, bonuses, executive pay, extra dollars, extra hours, extra rates, FICA limit reached in reversals, hourly employees, miscellaneous deductions, nontaxable earnings, normal rates, overtime hours, pay advances, payoffs, premium earnings, and so forth. We favor the alphabetical approach because it makes for fast retrieval of the kind of specific information an operator needs to do a specific job.

Other topics to be covered by a quick reference might include these:

- Before you begin (a confidence builder)
- Terms you should know (definitions of data processing terms that could not be avoided)
- Loading paper into the printer (highly graphic)

Introducing BETA

for the
operator

Some quick reading
to help you get started...

the
computer
operator

WORKBOOK

practice
exercises

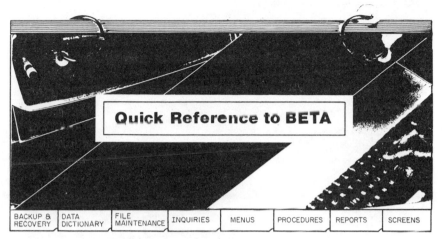

| BACKUP &
RECOVERY | DATA
DICTIONARY | FILE
MAINTENANCE | INQUIRIES | MENUS | PROCEDURES | REPORTS | SCREENS |

Fig. 6-6   Covers of some items included in an operator's kit. It is important to package these items in an attractive and highly graphic manner. (*Courtesy of International Business Machines Corporation*)

- Changing the printer's ribbon (also highly graphic)
- Signing on and off
- When you're stuck (troubleshooting procedures)

Another design of a quick reference is shown in Figure 6-8.

USER'S MANUALS

In the introduction to this book, we laid down some ground rules that we believe govern our ability to communicate clearly and effectively. It may be worthwhile to repeat six of them now, because in this section we show you how to apply these principles and others to the creation of major parts of a particular user's manual.

- Don't waste the beginning of the manual. Write it as though the reader will have only 20 minutes to give to the entire manual.
- Write to get the reader productive as soon as possible. The reader can't spare the time for a long period of learning.
- Respect the reader's time throughout the manual.
- Clear writing is simply good manners. Obscure writing is discourteous.

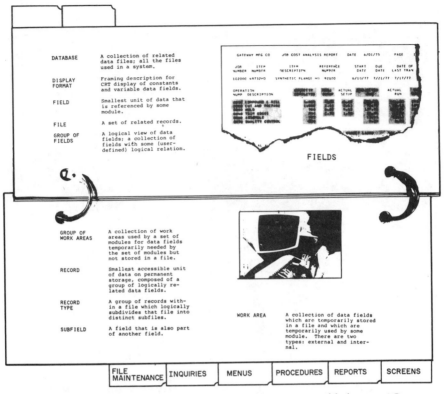

Fig. 6-7   A quick reference manual opened to show one possible layout. (*Courtesy of International Business Machines Corporation*)

- Don't merely *list* technical facts. Their connection to the reader must be clear.
- Bridge from the old to the new. Don't drop the reader into the middle of something new without explaining how it relates to his or her previous experience.

The user's manual from which the pages illustrated in Figures 6-9 to 6-18 are taken is intended to show a novice how to run a computer program that logs and keeps track of documents such as letters, memos, and reports. The manual is called *Document Logger*; the name Document Logger (abbreviated DL throughout the manual) is a short way of referring to this product. In the following pages we comment on these figures one by one. The figures are displayed on

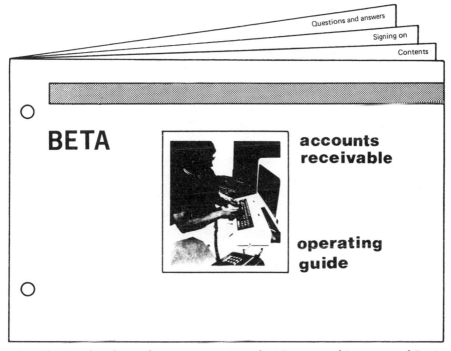

Fig. 6-8   Another design for an operator's guide. (*Courtesy of International Business Machines Corporation*)

consecutive pages to simulate the actual layout of the booklet. We urge you to turn to the designated figure as you read the accompanying commentary.

The cover of the booklet (Figure 6-9) illustrates the ground rule about not wasting the beginning of the manual. At once you see that the cover differs from what readers are accustomed to seeing with the usual manual. This cover (and the back cover, as you will see shortly) is not wasted. Instead of a typical preface introducing the manual, the cover contains a personal memo to the reader giving the advantages of the product. Why? For one thing, it's a nice touch, enabling the writer to use a graphic, but there are practical reasons too:

- It tells anyone who might pick up the booklet (including a potential customer) what the product does. The cover sells. For those who have already purchased the product, the cover resells.
- It's a friendly greeting to a possibly nervous person getting ready to

confront the computer. Note the warm feeling conveyed not only by the message but also by the handwritten signature.

- It serves the purpose of brevity, because it eliminates the page or two usually given to a preface or other introductory material.

The words "Instruction Booklet" immediately let the reader know exactly what class of publication it is and what it is for. With many publications, this is a guessing game. The word *booklet* implies that it is small, not an ordeal. The title *Document Logger* both specifies the product and its purpose. The language is short and simple. A TME (technical manual English) title might read something like *System/99 Document/Correspondence Logging Facility User's Guide*.

The table of contents (Figure 6-10) reveals the booklet's contents, not only by identifying the major sections but also by annotating the contents. Thus, the table of contents serves as a summary of the booklet, giving the reader a quick grasp of what's in the booklet.

Facing the table of contents page is the page headed "About reports" (Figure 6-11), which discusses and *shows* the main reports produced by the product. In most manuals, the results (such as reports) are usually reserved for discussion at the end. Here, the reader sees the results first, then has an explanation of how to get them. The whole purpose of acquiring the product is to get those results. Putting them first shows the reader the objective, the aim, the end result of what he or she is about to do. It's like pointing out a destination on a map. It lets the reader preview the results that can be expected. Thus, the reader has some idea of the reason behind every instruction in the booklet. It is important for people to have a sense of purpose, a sense of where they are going *before* they start out. Putting the reports first accomplishes that purpose.

This "touching base" with results need not be a long discussion, for when the reader turns the page, he or she sees that the introduction to reports ends (see Figure 6-12). So it's a *brief* introduction.

The page titled "Start it up" (Figure 6-13) is only the third page of the booklet. By the third page, the reader is already taking actions, doing something, moving forward, getting something accomplished. *Doing,* not just reading.

Remember the ground rule about writing all instructions in imperative language? All the instructions begin with verbs of com-

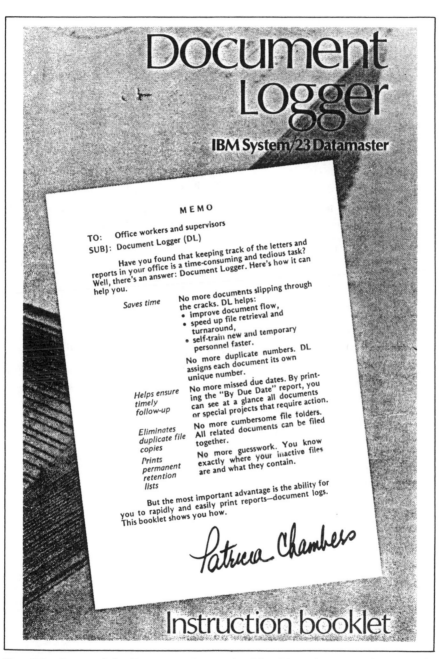

Fig. 6-9 Cover of the *Document Logger* booklet. Note the personal memo addressed to readers and potential customers. This product and its booklet are mythical, intended for instructional purposes only. (*Figures 6-9 to 6-18 are reprinted by permission from International Business Machines Corporation.*)

In this booklet

IBM®

Fig. 6-10   Inside front cover of the booklet.

About reports

No more searching through scribbled logs.
On request, DL prints reports by:

- document number
- author's name
- date written
- receiver's name
- keyword
- responder
- due date

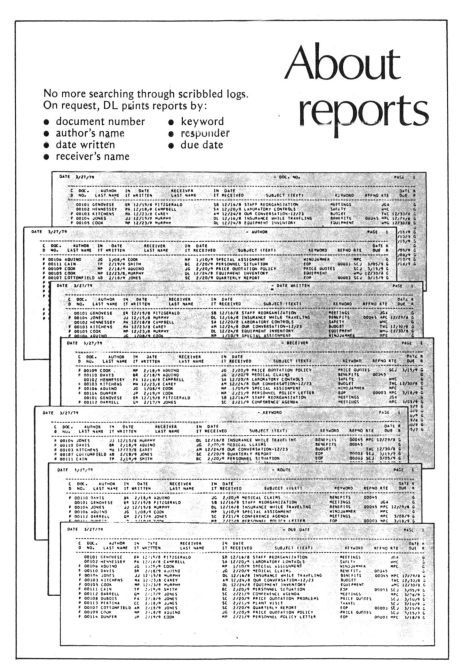

Fig. 6-11 Showing results early.

More about reports

Depending on your needs, you can select either a general or a specific report.

For each type, you can print reports for a certain 'from and to' period of time. Notice the order of the report columns always stays the same regardless of which type of report you select.

General reports

A general report is a list of all the log entries in:

numerical order by:
- document number
- date written
- due date

OR

alphabetical order based on:
- author's last name
- receiver's last name
- keyword
- responder's initials

Here's an example of a general report printed by due date:

Specific reports

A specific report is a list of a particular group of documents:
- written on a particular date
- addressed to a specific individual
- associated with a certain keyword
- routed to a specific individual
- due on a certain date

Here's an example of a list of correspondence addressed only to Ms Jones:

Fig. 6-12 Conclusion of a brief introduction.

138

Start it up

To get ready...

☐ Make sure you have taken the Datamaster operator training, *Learning to Use System/23*, form number SA34-0134.

☐ Make a copy of the MINLIB diskette. During the practice session, you'll alter the sample log we've created for you. Make a copy so that you'll always have a *master* copy for others who do the practice. Label the copy you make 'MINLIB Training' and use the current date.

☐ Make sure you have the following hardware and software:
- A Datamaster with a *double* diskette drive
- A printer
- A CSF diskette
- A BRADS diskette
- A MINLIB diskette
- Two extra diskettes (these can be blank or contain data you no longer need)

Follow these steps each time you use DL, whether you're printing reports, or just adding new log entries.

1. Put the CSF diskette into drive 1
2. Put the BRADS diskette into drive 2
3. Type in PROC INSTALL.MINI
4. Remove CSF diskette from drive 1 and insert MINLIB diskette in drive 1
5. Check to see that the printer has printed this message: SUCCESSFUL INSTALLATION
6. The ready input screen appears

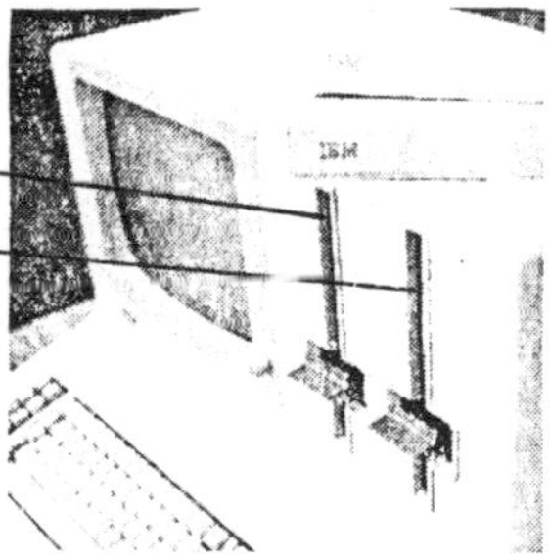

Now you're ready to practice using it.

Fig. 6-13 By the third page, the reader is *doing* the job.

Practice using it

Welcome to Office Industries!

For this practice you'll be running DL for Office Industries, a sample company we've created for you. You will learn DL by using Office Industries documents. That way, you can practice the DL jobs using this information first — before using it with your company's real documents.

Here are all the things you're going to do with DL:

- print a report
- add an entry to the log
- change a log entry
- erase an entry
- copy your log onto a backup diskette
- restore your log
- erase log entries from the diskette

We want you to be at ease during the practice; so before you begin, review the 'What if' section on the inside back cover. It may answer some questions that could come up during practice.

Pull out the foldout in the back of the booklet and *leave it folded out*. It shows the screens you will be working with as you follow the instructions for using DL.

Fig. 6-14 Beginning of the scenario.

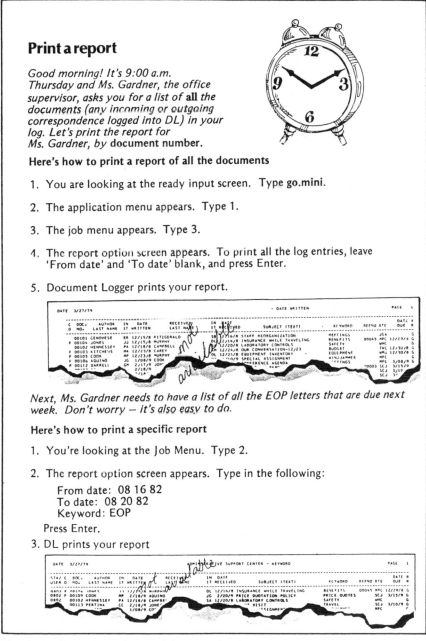

Print a report

Good morning! It's 9:00 a.m.
Thursday and Ms. Gardner, the office
supervisor, asks you for a list of all the
documents (any incoming or outgoing
correspondence logged into DL) in your
log. Let's print the report for
Ms. Gardner, by document number.

Here's how to print a report of all the documents

1. You are looking at the ready input screen. Type **go.mini**.

2. The application menu appears. Type 1.

3. The job menu appears. Type 3.

4. The report option screen appears. To print all the log entries, leave 'From date' and 'To date' blank, and press Enter.

5. Document Logger prints your report.

Next, Ms. Gardner needs to have a list of all the EOP letters that are due next week. Don't worry — it's also easy to do.

Here's how to print a specific report

1. You're looking at the Job Menu. Type 2.

2. The report option screen appears. Type in the following:

    From date: 08 16 82
    To date: 08 20 82
    Keyword: EOP

    Press Enter.

3. DL prints your report

Fig. 6-15 Scenario tied in with learning by doing.

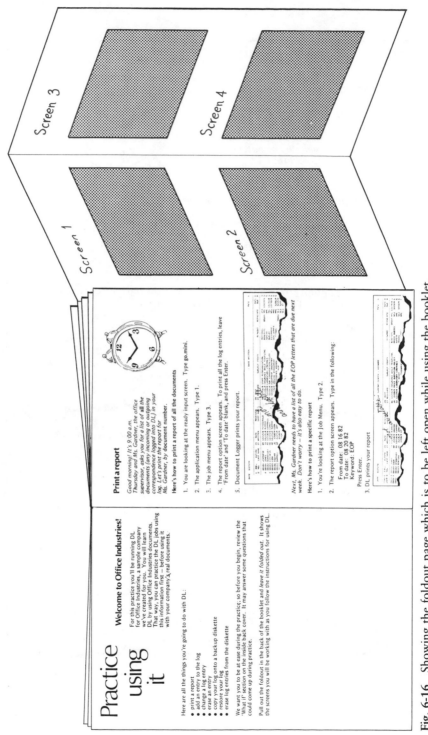

Fig. 6-16 Showing the foldout page which is to be left open while using the booklet.

☐ select a filing system

Document Logger has three filing systems:

- numeric
- reference
- subject

You can use one system for all your documents or a combination of subject and numeric.

Numeric. In numeric filing, DL assigns a sequential number to each document you enter. You write that number on the document and file it in numeric sequence. This makes filing of your documents simple, because you don't have to decide which subjects to file them under.

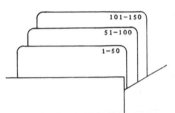

Reference. In reference filing, you file all related documents together. For example, a letter comes in regarding a dental claim for G. Johnson. DL assigns it a document number of 20. Later a follow-up letter about this claim is received. DL assigns it a number of 40. Since it refers to document number 20, type 20 in the reference column. Write 20 and 40 at the top of the letter and circle 20. Both the claim and the letter are filed under 20. Any further correspondence referring to G. Johnson's dental claim is handled the same way—regardless of individually assigned document numbers.

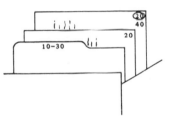

With this system, duplicate filing is reduced. There's no need to keep separate subject, numeric or follow-up files.

Even if a document does not refer to previous correspondence (a letter that doesn't need a response), reference filing can be used.

Fig. 6-17 Bridging from old to new by illustrations of opened file drawers.

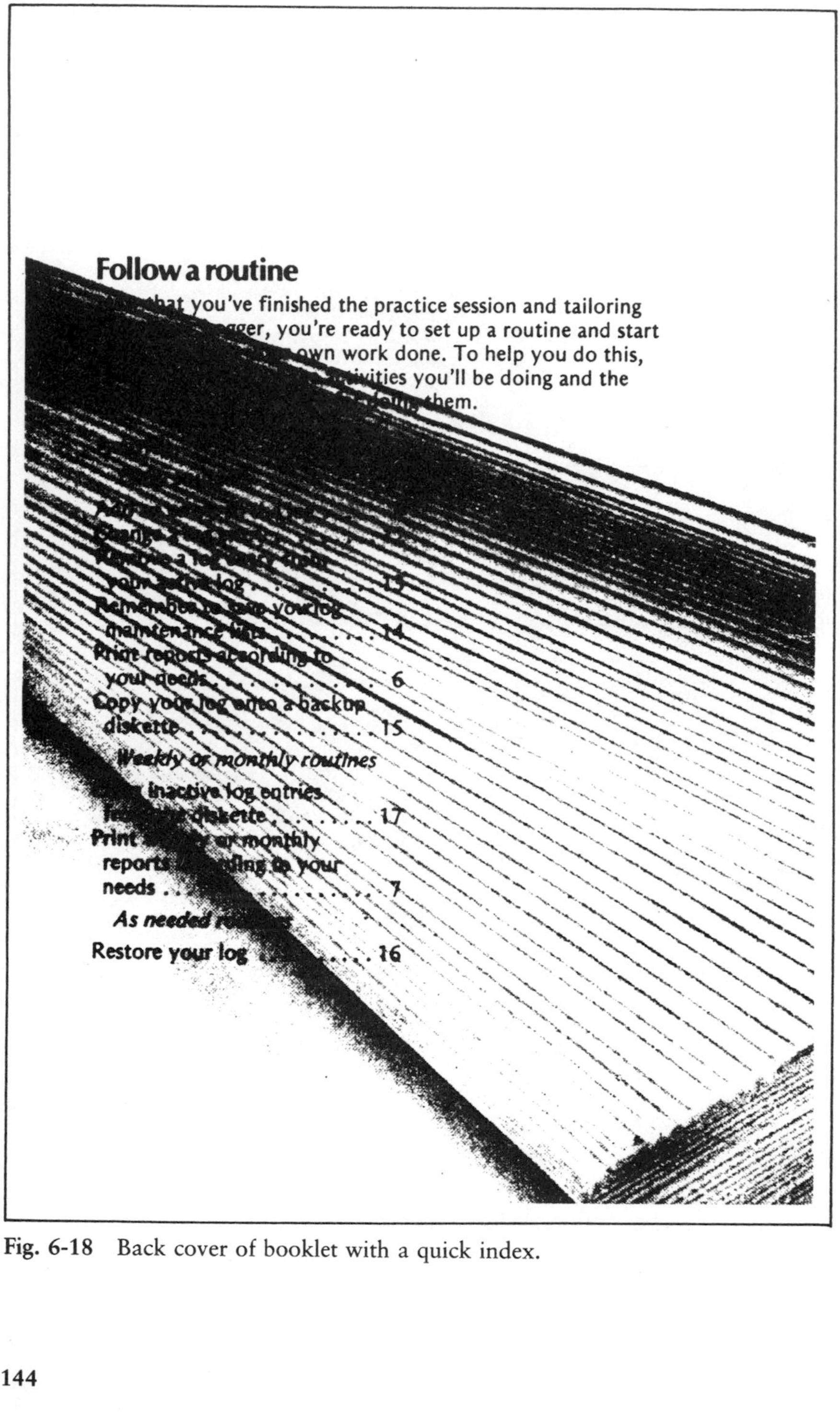

Follow a routine

...that you've finished the practice session and tailoring
...ger, you're ready to set up a routine and start
...own work done. To help you do this,
...ivities you'll be doing and the
...them.

Fig. 6-18   Back cover of booklet with a quick index.

mand—*put, type, remove,* and so forth. The instructions avoid the all-too-common passive voice such as "Diskette CP-W should be put in drive 1."

Remember the ground rule about showing the reader how to do it? The arrows from steps 1 and 2 point to the machine, *showing* the reader where to put the diskettes.

Immediately following the start-it-up page are several pages of instructions that allow the reader to practice procedures before attempting the real thing. Figures 6-14 and 6-15 show the first two pages of this section.

At this point we want to introduce the idea of the scenario as a training technique. When you first learned to drive, you were not taken into downtown traffic for your first lessons. You probably were taken to some large empty area where there was no traffic and therefore little risk of collision. The person who first uses a computer program in a business setting needs a similar feeling of security. He or she wants to know that any mistakes made in learning how to perform a procedure will not destroy the company's records or do other damage. To accomplish this, use the scenario—a simulation of what the reader will be doing with the product or procedure once he or she has mastered how to use it. The scenario exercises the learner—without risk—in every job the product does.

The scenario that starts on the pages illustrated in Figures 6-14 and 6-15 simulates a typical workday, from morning until quitting time. Thus, the learner can identify with the activities explained in the scenario. Learning the procedure becomes real, not a series of abstract, irrelevant, purposeless tasks. When the reader reaches the end of the booklet, he or she will have "lived through" a typical workday, learning by *doing.* All that remains is to "go live."

Remember the ground rule about respecting the reader's time? One of the key strategies that keeps the booklet small begins with the last statement on the page illustrated in Figure 6-14:

> Pull out the foldout in the back of the booklet and *leave it folded out.* It shows the screens you will be working with as you follow the instructions for using DL.

Reproducing all the screens at the points where they are mentioned would have at least doubled the page count of the booklet. The strategy is to select the four most important screens and put them on a foldout page at the end of the booklet. While the reader is following the instructions, he or she leaves that foldout page open in order to refer to a screen. The booklet with the foldout page extended is shown in Figure 6-16. As the ground rule says, omit information that the reader is likely to know. Showing every screen as it is mentioned would waste the reader's time, especially since the screens are so similar in content and appearance.

The page that explains how to select a filing system (Figure 6-17) illustrates with words and pictures how to bridge from the old to the new, from the known to the unknown. To explain filing by computer, the writer relates it to older methods of filing by hand. The graphics on this page show open file drawers with records sticking out. The reader sees something familiar that he or she can relate to.

The back cover (Figure 6-18) allows the opportunity to say something useful. After all, a manual may lie on its front cover a good part of the time, making the back cover available for some worthwhile purpose. The back cover is not wasted here. It offers a chance for a parting shot—a list of reminders, a final word of advice, a handy index of main topics, whatever best suits your purpose.

ON-LINE DOCUMENTATION

We are moving rapidly toward a day when the computer itself will teach the operator how to run it. That is, the computer screen will be used to display all the instructions the computer operator needs to operate the computer. Indeed, there already exist programs that ask operators questions in much the same way that a psychotherapist talks to a patient.

Putting instructions for running a program on a computer screen, information that ordinarily would be published in a traditional manual, is called by various names, among them *on-line documentation*.

Data processing professionals hold differing opinions regarding on-line documentation, but most believe that the day is coming when advanced technology will enable us to use on-line documentation exclusively.

Those who question the feasibility of on-line documentation are concerned about four points.

- Under the present state of the art, much computer graphics lack the realism and resolution of pictures in print and on video.

- A trainee or a backup operator can review a traditional manual at any time it's convenient. They cannot, however, use a computer for review or training while that computer terminal is on-line for business purposes. You can't take a terminal home and read it.

- On-line text ties up a substantial amount of computer storage over extended periods of time for explanatory material that may be used only once by a trainee.

- To communicate through on-line documentation—a tool radically different from the traditional user's manual—requires a different expertise. Just as you cannot use a radio script on television or a television script on radio, you cannot use the prose of traditional documentation on a computer screen. The computer is a significantly different communication medium, and you have to change the presentation to match.

Those who see the evidence piling up that we are on the way to overcoming the limitations of on-line documentation cite the following eight points.

- The only thing that can keep up with the speed of the machine is the machine itself. An operator cannot keep up with the speed of the computer while flipping the pages of a written document. He or she is always out of sync, never able to catch up or find what is needed. Putting the information on-line enables the operator to retrieve information at electronic speed.

- In today's business world, there is an increasing reluctance to read technical manuals . . . for a variety of reasons. Technical manuals have acquired a reputation of being too dull, too time-consuming, too hard, full of jargon, and over the heads of their intended audiences. People today want to receive information faster and in a more graphic and interesting form, a medium that reminds them of television.

- The economics and logistics of producing, distributing, and maintaining conventional technical manuals are becoming prohibitive.

- It is only a matter of time before hardware technology will offer animation in color. It will then be possible to explain very difficult subjects—like system control—in a manner that can be understood by non-data processing professionals.

- There are psychological considerations and human factors that should be weighed. We have only to observe the crush of people in an arcade of video games to appreciate the appeal of the tube—a graphic device offering immediate feedback—to all ages and classes of people. (In effect, millions of people have already been on-line without knowing it.) We should take advantage of this aspect of human nature in our own product conveyance, to communicate more effectively to the new audience for our products: the lay user.

- In yesterday's data processing, things happened in a more or less sequential and fairly predictable order. Knowing that order, we could write a document to match a step-by-step sequence of events which the operator could follow. In today's data processing, things happen in dynamic and unpredictable sequences. No document can capture these dynamics. Only the machine can keep up with itself and be a guide to the operator.

- A person learns to drive a car by actually driving it, not by reading a manual. The same thing is true of any machine, including a computer. The best vehicle for teaching how to operate a computer is the computer itself.

- "Can our people handle it?" is the question uppermost in the minds of business owners contemplating computers. By putting the operator guidance and other material on-line, we will reduce the negative effect created by a stack of technical manuals which says to the readers: "This is very complicated. Maybe too complicated for you."

We believe that we cannot ignore or dismiss the development of on-line documentation that is assuredly taking place. Now that it is being established, we believe its use will develop even faster. But we also believe that before it can develop further, one of the most important features of operator and machine dialogue must be improved—the menu.

We all know what a restaurant menu is. It lists the items of food available (hopefully) for your selection in that establishment. Similarly, the computer menu is a list of items, displayed on the computer's screen, from which the operator selects what he or she wants the computer to do. An example of such an item is "Print the payroll checks."

The idea of the menu was a great step forward in the technology of communicating with the computer. It enables inexperienced people to use the computer with less difficulty than presented by the previous method. With the previous method, one would type in a list of parameters, or code words. Thus, to command the computer to print payroll checks, the operator would have to type in something like

PR,,,,421,EXEC,,17,RRR/NN

Memorizing such codes, or looking them up, was a chore, especially since many of the codes were not constructed so as to make remembering them easy. To take that same action now, the operator merely selects a number from a list of items on a menu, for instance:

1. XXXXXXXXXXXXXXXXXXXX.
2. XXXXXXXXXXXXXXXXXXXX.
3. XXXXXXXXXXXXXXXXXXXX.
4. Print payroll checks.
5. XXXXXXXXXXXXXXXXXXXX.

All the operator has to do is hit two keys—4 and EXECUTE, or some similar command.

Easy enough and fast enough. But how should the menus for complicated programs be designed from the standpoint of good communication? Generally speaking, there are two fundamental approaches to designing computer menus: the multilevel approach and the single-level approach.

In the multilevel approach (Figure 6-19), there is a main menu, a secondary menu (maybe even a tertiary menu), and a final screen for adding or changing data. Let's say, for example, that an operator wants to delete (erase) a customer's record from the file of customer records. The operator must first select item 6 of the main menu. The main menu disappears, replaced by the secondary menu. The opera-

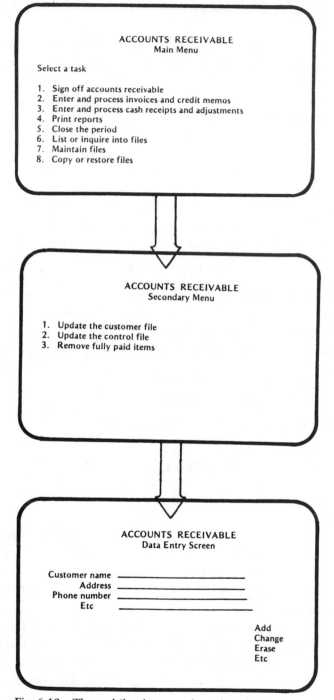

Fig. 6-19 The multilevel approach, with a main menu and a secondary menu.

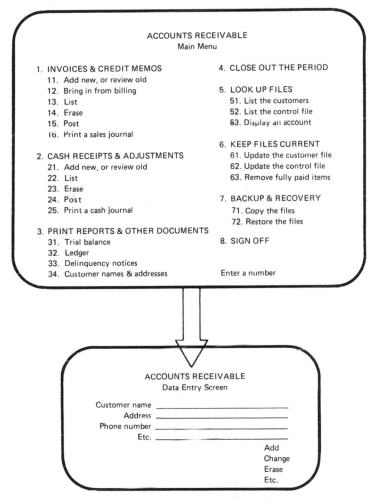

ACCOUNTS RECEIVABLE
Main Menu

1. INVOICES & CREDIT MEMOS
   11. Add new, or review old
   12. Bring in from billing
   13. List
   14. Erase
   15. Post
   16. Print a sales journal

2. CASH RECEIPTS & ADJUSTMENTS
   21. Add new, or review old
   22. List
   23. Erase
   24. Post
   25. Print a cash journal

3. PRINT REPORTS & OTHER DOCUMENTS
   31. Trial balance
   32. Ledger
   33. Delinquency notices
   34. Customer names & addresses

4. CLOSE OUT THE PERIOD

5. LOOK UP FILES
   51. List the customers
   52. List the control file
   53. Display an account

6. KEEP FILES CURRENT
   61. Update the customer file
   62. Update the control file
   63. Remove fully paid items

7. BACKUP & RECOVERY
   71. Copy the files
   72. Restore the files

8. SIGN OFF

Enter a number

ACCOUNTS RECEIVABLE
Data Entry Screen

Customer name _____
Address _____
Phone number _____
Etc. _____

Add
Change
Erase
Etc.

Fig. 6-20 The single-level approach, where the operator goes straight from the main menu to the job at hand.

tor then selects item 1 of the secondary menu. That menu disappears, replaced by the final screen. The final screen enables the operator to make the actual change (erase a record) that was the goal in the first place.

In the single-level approach (Figure 6-20), the computer displays a list not only of the broad categories of work but also of the final jobs themselves. Thus, instead of going through a main menu and a secondary menu—and maybe even lower levels of menus—the operator

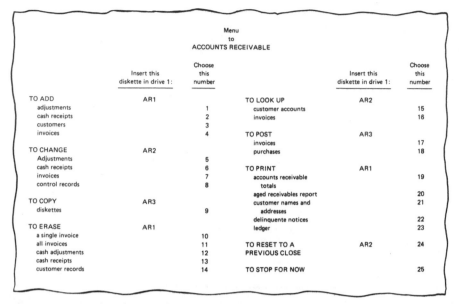

Fig. 6-21   Another design of the single-level menu. Note the verbs of *action: add, change,* and so on.

goes straight to the job at hand, in this case erasing a customer's record.

Obviously, there are fewer items to select from in each menu of the multilevel approach. So each menu is less crowded. However, with the multilevel approach, the operator has to refer to some source, such as a technical publication, to be *sure* that he or she is making the right selection from the main menu and perhaps from the secondary one as well. Remember, each menu disappears as soon as the operator makes a selection from it. If the operator selects the wrong item from the main menu, the secondary menu will be the wrong one. And that means that the operator will have to find the way back to the main menu and try another selection.

In contrast to that uncertainty, we can see from Figure 6-20 that to get to the final screen of the single-level menu, the operator merely selects item 61. And the operator immediately gets the screen that enables him or her to do the job (erase the customer's record).

We conclude that the single-level menu approach is more efficient and less prone to error, because it allows the operator to see the entire procedure at one time and it lets the operator get to the end result without going through levels and sublevels of menus that unnecessarily fragment the procedure.

Shown in Figure 6-21 is another version of the single-level menu design. In this example we are really communicating in the language of the lay user. We are accommodating that person's view of the task at hand by using terms such as *add, delete,* and so forth. Note the absence of terms historically connected with data processing: *input, output, function,* and the like.

This final section of Chapter 6 has dealt with on-line documentation, something that we are moving closer to having, both in the workplace and at home. However, until the use of on-line documentation is widespread, the need for good technical manuals remains crucial. Even after on-line documentation becomes the norm, the principles of communication that we have presented throughout this book remain the same regardless of the medium in which the ideas are expressed. Incomprehensible prose and graphics displayed on a computer screen remain incomprehensible prose and graphics.

Index

ABOUT THE AUTHORS

Gerald Cohen has had twenty years of experience as a technical writer and editor. He has worked for IBM for several years, teaching technical writing in that company's voluntary education programs, and he has traveled nationwide to conduct seminars and presentations on technical writing. He is a guest lecturer at the Technical Writing Institute of Rensselaer Polytechnic Institute.

Donald H. Cunningham, professor of English and director of technical and professional writing at Texas Tech University, is involved with many communications organizations. A speaker at workshops and seminars and a contract writer for business, industry, and government, his recent books include *The Practical Craft: Readings for Business and Technical Writers* (with W. Keats Sparrow) and *How to Write for the World of Work* (with Thomas E. Pearsall). This is his tenth year as editor of *The Technical Writing Teacher*.